THE PENGUIN CLASSICS

EDITED BY E. V. RIEU

L 128

CONFESSIO AMANTIS

[THE LOVER'S SHRIFT]

John Gower

*Translated into Modern English
with an Introduction by*
TERENCE TILLER

PENGUIN BOOKS
BALTIMORE · MARYLAND

Penguin Books Ltd, Harmondsworth, Middlesex
U.S.A.: Penguin Books Inc., 3300 Clipper Mill Road, Baltimore 11, Md
AUSTRALIA: Penguin Books Pty Ltd, 762 Whitehorse Road,
Mitcham, Victoria

—

This translation first published 1963

—

Copyright © Terence Tiller, 1963

—

Made and printed in Great Britain
by C. Nicholls & Company Ltd
Set in Monotype Garamond

/

Contents

Titles in italics indicate that the story is given only, or mainly, in prose summary.

CONTENTS

CONTENTS

CONTENTS

Introduction

NOT a great deal is known, for certain, about Gower's life; we know far more about Chaucer, and scarcely less about Shakespeare. This is due in part to the apparent existence, during the poet's lifetime, of one or two namesakes: not every 'John Gower' document necessarily refers to our author. We are sure of his marriage licence, of his will, and of his tomb in Southwark. We know that his friend Chaucer gave him a general power-of-attorney (jointly with one Richard Forester) when Sir Edward Berkeley took Chaucer on a diplomatic mission to Lombardy, in 1378. That Chaucer *was* Gower's friend, we further know from a reference in *Confessio Amantis* itself, from Chaucer's dedication of *Troilus and Cryseyde,* and from Chaucer's comment upon Gower's tale of Canace (Introduction to the *Man of Law's Tale,* l.77). Certain documents exist which granted Gower lands and privileges. And that is virtually all.

The date of his birth is unknown but was probably between 1327 and 1330. He came of a good Kentish family: the manor of Kentwell, in Suffolk, eventually reverted to him from his kinsman Sir Robert Gower. With a social origin of this kind, he had access to Court circles: by his own account, he was known personally to the King; and certainly he received from the hand of Richard II the rectory of Great Braxted in Essex, which he occupied from 1390 to 1397. It is certain – from the fact of his marriage – that he was not however a priest. The tradition that he and Chaucer were both members of the Inner Temple is probably untrue: Gower hated lawyers. On the other hand, he seems never – or very

9

briefly – to have lived upon his various lands; and they were many. In 1382 he acquired both Feltwell, in Norfolk, and Moulton, in Suffolk. His Kentish holdings were in Throwley, Stalesfield, and Aldington. His own country house, in Kent, was at Otford. In addition, he drew rents from Wigborough in Essex. We may conjecture, then, that he was a man of sufficient means to live a town-life, part courtier and part scholar, as a kind of absentee landlord.

It appears likely that he was not much at Court: he was a man of simple tastes, and shows a predilection for the common man, profoundly though he hated Wycliffe and the Lollards. Moreover, his industry as a writer (see below) was considerable, his health poor; and we know that he lived for many years, retired, in the Priory of St Mary Overies, Southwark, to which he was a considerable benefactor both during his life and in his will. So that although, in 1393 or later, he was given by Henry of Lancaster – Bolingbroke – the collar which his tomb-effigy shows him wearing, he cannot have been the courtier and man of affairs that Chaucer was.

In 1397 he resigned his rectory of Braxted and appears to have abandoned worldly intercourse. Though aged, in this year he married Agnes Groundolf – undoubtedly as a nurse – and lived with her thenceforth in the Priory. In 1408 he drew up his will, and died later in the same year. It is believed that he had been blind for several years before his death.

WORKS

Gower is unique among English poets in that his three major works, and a number of minor works and fragments, are in three different languages. *Confessio Amantis* is in English; *Vox Clamantis* ('The Voice of One Crying') in Latin; *Speculum Meditantis* ('The Mirror of One Meditating') in French. These form a very considerable corpus – *Confessio Amantis* alone runs to about

30,000 lines, 6,000 more than *The Canterbury Tales* – and the bias of them all is moralistic; though it must be admitted that some tales in *Confessio Amantis* (as Chaucer himself thought) do not immediately strike one as moral.

Of the three, it is *Confessio Amantis* that shows most originality and contains most genuine poetry. Gower's Latin, full as it is of plagiarisms, is fluent but a little unwieldy; his French, that of the Court, is elegant but somewhat artificial. His English is alive, with Kentish forms and locutions breaking through the Court English which he almost – but not quite – shares with Chaucer. *Vox Clamantis*, inspired by the Jack Straw Rebellion of 1381, is an impassioned plea for established order, justice for all men however humble, and a Church purified of its manifold corruptions. This distress is manifested also in the Prologue to *Confessio Amantis*, and in those passages where the Confessor inveighs against unjust governors or corrupt churchmen. But the chief interest of *Confessio Amantis* – apart from the stories themselves – perhaps lies in its ingenious treatment of the conventions of courtly love (see C. S. Lewis, *The Allegory of Love*, Oxford, 1936) within the apparently alien framework of the Seven Deadly Sins.

At first sight, this framework is an unpromising device for stringing together stories of widely different character; and, indeed, the mechanism does creak somewhat on occasion. Venus appoints her Chaplain, Genius by name, to hear Gower confess his sins against the laws of Love; the Chaplain – with elaborate subdivisions worthy of Dante – treats each of the Seven Deadly Sins in turn, first from the purely Christian standpoint, then from that of the Courts of Love; and he illustrates most points with at least one story. This method reduces Genius to the anomalous position of – for instance – defending incest against the Church, and virginity against that goddess whose Chaplain he is. Derived partly from Chaucer, partly from the *Roman de la Rose* (in which also we find a Chaplain called Genius), Gower's idea was in some ways less effective than either.

Even so, it works. And the occasional cumbrousness is amply paid for by the very human characters that emerge, of the Lover and his Lady. We are given not only the medieval *conventions* of love, but vignette after vignette of medieval life as it really was. Gower seldom describes people with Chaucer's vivid minuteness; but his characters do 'come alive'.

It was at one time the fashion to compare Gower and Chaucer much in the manner of the school examinee comparing Keats and Shelley. This is an unrewarding pastime, for Gower's aims were quite different from those of his friend: more modest, more sober, more serious. Gower has less wit and humour, less drama and panache, not only by nature but also by choice. Nevertheless, these qualities are by no means absent. And, when he chooses, Gower can rise to real eloquence and splendour – as in his many descriptions of weather, or in the 'Prayer of Cephalus' and the 'Tale of Ceyx and Halcyone' (both in Book Four). He is capable of real pathos, as in the 'Tale of Canace' (Book Three), and of genuine excitement, as in the 'Tale of Medea' (Book Five). His most remarkable quality, however, is his tireless ease and fluency – all in meticulous rhyme and metre – while avoiding both monotony and 'bittiness'. He was a lesser poet; but he was, in his chosen way, almost as great a craftsman as was Chaucer in his.

TEXTS, TRANSLATION, ETC.

Some forty manuscripts of *Confessio Amantis* are known to exist. There are two distinct versions, differing mainly in the Prologue and at the end. The earliest form is internally dated 1390; the second, with its new dedication to Henry of Lancaster, 1392-3. A third, intermediate, version shows a partial return to the first form, but with again rewritten passages. This is not the place in which to embark upon detailed comparisons. I have almost exclusively used for my translation the text adopted by G. C. Macaulay (Oxford, 1901) as his basis; this is MS. Fairfax 3. I have ignored the – often extensive and prolonged – variant passages.

Early printed editions reflect, in their number, the extraordinary popularity that Gower enjoyed for at least two centuries. *Confessio Amantis* was very soon translated into both Spanish and Portuguese; Caxton printed a composite version in 1483; Gower appears as a 'narrator' in the partly Shakespearian *Pericles, Prince of Tyre* (which was itself adapted from a story in *Confessio Amantis*). But, with the exception of Macaulay's, there have been few really satisfactory editions of the original. Morley's in particular (Routledge, 1889) is a model of bad editing. As far as I know, there is no edition of the original currently in print.

'Translations' from Middle English are not as easy as may be supposed. Gower, even more than Chaucer, employs *rimes riches* that would not be acceptable in modern English verse: for example, 'Kepe' (verb) and 'Kepe' (noun). Inversions, also, though common enough in earlier verse, are rightly frowned upon today. This kind of difficulty, among others perhaps less obvious, must somehow be overcome in a 'translation' rather than a mere 'modernization'. Yet if the translation is to be of any practical use it must be as literal as possible – and as close as possible to the *spirit* of the original. Purely modern locutions, then, are to be avoided: 'it's a priest's job' will not do for 'it sit a prest'. What is needed is *neutral* English, neither unashamedly modern nor affectedly archaic.

I have not been able to adhere strictly to these ideals; on occasion I have had to compromise. One notable, and recurring, instance is the use of the second person singular. Gower, out of respect, always addresses the

Confessor as 'you'; the Confessor calls Gower 'thou'. Since this distinction is deliberate, and in accordance with fourteenth-century social usage, I have retained it. Now and then I have employed slightly archaic – 'poetic' – turns of phrase; or inversions. On the whole, however, I have tried to use the equivalent of that natural and neutral – albeit, often, very colloquial – English which Gower himself employed. Similarly, I have tried in the main to produce a line-for-line literal translation; but now and then I have allowed myself to change line order, or to paraphrase unmanageable sequences. This will not often be found to occur; and the paraphrases or 'displacements' never exceed half a dozen lines or so. Occasionally I have permitted myself – as Gower would never have done – an imperfect rhyme or a metrical licence.

The poem has been cut by me to about one-third of its original length. Excised passages are always summarized in prose, and their precise extent indicated, with two general exceptions: I have ignored the Latin marginal glosses, and the Latin verse summaries that are occasionally set at the heads of books and of major divisions, and at the end. Numbers in the margin refer to the line-count of the *original*.

Certain passages formed the basis of six short broadcasts in the Third Programme, during 1956. These have been almost entirely re-written – and for the most part, of course, greatly expanded; but my thanks are due to the B.B.C. for permission to print them.

TERENCE TILLER

Prologue

Of those who wrote in days of yore,
The books remain, and we therefore
May learn by what was written then.
Thus it is fit that living men
Should also in this latter age
Find some new subject for their page,
(Though copied from the tales of old)
If it be cast in such a mould
That when we die and go elsewhere
It lingers on the wide world's ear   10
In times to follow after this.
Only, men say – and truth it is –
That works of wholly solemn kind
Will often dull a reader's mind,
Who studies in them every day;
So I will walk the middle way,
If you advise me so to do,
And write a book between the two –
Something to please, something to profit –
So that the most or least part of it   20
May give some readers some delight.
And furthermore, since few men write
In our English, I think to make
One book at least for England's sake.

King Richard's sixteenth year it is;
And what will happen after this,
God knows – for men see nowadays,
Whichever way they turn their gaze,
The world so changed and overthrown
That it is well-nigh upside down   30
Compared with days of long ago.

The reason why it changes so,
There is no need to specify:
So plain and open to the eye
It is, that all men may behold.
Nevertheless, in days of old,
When books were better loved by men,
Writing was honourable then
To all whose lives were virtuous.
40 Here in this world, as touching *us* –
If no man wrote how matters stood,
The fame of such as had been good
Would largely (as the saying goes)
Be lost. And so, for praising those
Most worthy princes of the past,
Books are exemplars first and last,
To show the world what virtue is.
Men who in those days did amiss
Through tyranny and cruelty –
50 Such as each was, in his degree,
So upon history stands his mark.
Thus I, who am a homespun clerk,
Am purposing to write a book
About the way the old world took
A long time since, in former days:
But, seeing how the world decays –
Its plight much worse than long ago –
I plan to make my theme also
The world new-fashioned every day;
60 If I but can, if I but may.
Though sicknesses upon me lie,
And long have lain, yet I shall try
To write, as duty says I must;
So that some part of it, I trust,
May be of profit to the wise.
For thus my Prologue I devise,
That all to wisdom I devote it:
If a wise man receive and note it,

16

Within himself he shall recall
How the world's luck and fortune fall   70
(But why they do so is not known
To any mind but God's alone).
And when this Prologue is complete,
The body of my book shall treat
Of love, that many a wise man brings
To grief, and does amazing things.
And thus I purpose to discuss
Those set in greatness over us,
And weigh the righteousness and wrong
Which to such offices belong.   80
But, as my knowledge is too small
To keep a proper count of all
Men's 'good' and 'bad', this book I send –
For his commandment to amend –
Unto my own and liegest lord,
With whom my heart is in accord:
Henry of Lancaster his name;
And him the High God doth proclaim
Pattern of knighthood and all grace.
So will I now this work embrace,   90
Firmly both trusting and believing;
God grant me power for its achieving.

If I shall summon to my mind
Those olden days, then I shall find
How all the world was full of wealth:
The life of man was passed in health;
Riches and plenty flourished then;
Then fortune favoured valiant men;
Knighthood was then an honoured name
Whereof, world-wide, men wrote the fame   100
In chronicles that still endure;
Then law and justice were secure,
The privilege of royalty
Upheld, and all the barony

Respected in their high estate.
The cities were not in debate,
The people were subservient
Under the rule of government;
And peace, by righteousness caressed,
110 With charity lay down in rest.
Men let their countenance express
Their secret hearts and inwardness;
No manner of deceit was wrought,
The word was mirror to the thought;
Then love was safe from jealousy;
Then virtue was prized royally,
And vice was trampled underfoot.
Now lies the flower below the root;
The world has altered utterly,
120 And in one way especially:
Love has grown all discordant now.
And, for your witness, set down how
In every land beneath the sky,
With common voice which cannot lie
(Not one by one but all for all
It is that now they cry and call),
Men say their kingdoms are divided;
By hate, not love, are laws decided;
No peace is now the prize of war;
130 The law is double-faced, therefore
All justice now has lost its way
And righteousness is gone astray.
And thus on all sides is revealed
That ulcer which is never healed
And which is borne by everyone.
Kingdom or climate, there is none
But has its share of pain to feel
As this or that way turns the wheel
(Which blindfold Fortune still revolves)
140 Whose meaning no man surely solves.
God only knows what's to be done;

But we who dwell beneath the moon
Live in a world by conflicts torn;
And chiefly if the power borne
By those who are the nations' guides
Have not good counsel from all sides,
To hold it upright so that Hate
Breaks not Love's orderly estate
(Which is the prime necessity
To keep a realm from anarchy):   150
This is the path all reason treads,
That unto them who are the heads,
The limbs should bow obedience,
And heads must praise and recompense
Their troth, and make them hearty cheer,
For good advice is good to hear;
And though one man alone be wise,
With twelve men wisdom multiplies.
And if the parties could agree,
Soon there were cause to hope that we   160
Might feel the grace of God descend
To bring this conflict to an end,
Though day by day it grows anew –
A thing that we should deeply rue,
And mostly for the sake of Christ
Whose very life was sacrificed
To give all people peacefulness.
But now men tell us, none the less,
That love has fled away from us,
And peace is ill-divided thus   170
Among the men who live today.
Oh, try the question every way:
He who loves reason, and would seek it
(I use the word as all men speak it),
Cannot but marvel at that fight
Whose victor no man knows aright.
For every land is self-deceived
And by its proper dole is grieved,

And yet men pay no heed at all.
180 But He before Whom all should fall,
To Whom there is no secret thing
In earthly minds' imagining:
May He cure all the ills and smarts
That trouble full and faithful hearts,
And bring Love back to us again;
May He, the lord and sovereign
Of this our worldly government,
Now mightily be provident
To seal His peace upon all lands
190 And take their cause into His hands,
So that the world may be appeased,
And His high Godhead too be pleased!

Lo, now, consider and behold
The life of clerks in days of old.
I have heard said that they were then
The guide and pattern of all men
Who sought the power that wisdom brings.
And first they prayed the King of Kings
That in the substance of their schooling
200 He would preserve them from befooling
Their wits with books of worldly mark,
Unfitting the degree of clerk,
And that they might eschew that vice
Which them, like Simon,* could entice
To take a fee into their hand.
For at that time, I understand,
The Lombard† used no banker's tricks
To buy or sell the bishoprics;
No letters then to write or carry

* This is Simon Magus, who tried to purchase the gift of the Holy Ghost, and so gave simony its name. See also l. 439.

† Lombard bankers were often employed as intermediaries in the buying and selling of preferment. The 'letters' mentioned are probably papal despatches dealing with the same kind of transaction.

For prebend or for dignitary,   210
Whether with parish or without;
The Church Key then stood not in doubt
Of earthly arms and warlike men,
And was no prize of battle then.
For those clerks did not think it right
To fall to quarrelling or fight;
But patience and simplicity
They welcomed, in the days gone by;
In those days they thought alien things
The courts and powers of earthly Kings: 220
That with which many proud hearts fire,
Vain honour, was not their desire;
For pride among such men was deemed
A vice, humility esteemed.
Then, Holy Church was liberal
And gave and did great alms to all
Poor men, or such as stood in need.
Then clerks were chaste in word and deed,
A model for their flocks to heed;
All their desire was but to read   230
The Bible, or to preach, or pray,
And teach the straight and narrow way
To all whose sight of truth was bleared.
Thus was the Ship of Peter* steered
By those who were its masters then;
Thus first there reached the ears of men
The faith of Christ and all its good:
Through sober men, and chaste, who stood
For virtue, wisdom, bounty. How
The times are altered for us now!   240
Now Simony has come to Court,
And weapons are the world's resort –
Whereof our wonder may not cease
(When Christ Himself commanded peace
And set it in His Testament),

* The Church.

Now Holy Church grows dissident
From her own law, Law Positive,*
And sets about to war and strive
For worldly goods that soon are lost.
250 God knows indeed the uttermost
Of right and wrong in every cause;
But while men so apply the laws
That clerks themselves to war descend,
I know not how they will amend
This woeful world in other things –
As to bring peace among its Kings
After the laws of charity,
Which is an office properly
Belonging to the priesthood. Still,
260 It seems to human thought and will
That heaven is far, while earth is nigh;
And Vainglory has grown so sly,
With Greed for his companion,
That other object have they none,
But only to increase their gain.
And thus they fall to strife again,
For which the Holy Church must pay;
Even the tithes, the moment they
Are asked for, make men violent –
270 As if our Lord were impotent
To give a different reward.
The church key has become a sword;
What was at one time holy prayer
Is turned to cursing; everywhere
That men are steady in the creed
And give the matter any heed,
They are amazed by this ill-feeling.
What should have blessed the world with healing
Has now become a foul disease
280 Which drives all patience overseas –

* *Lex positiva* – law imposed by ecclesiastical authority, but not
in itself necessarily a *moral* obligation.

22

From clergy in particular.
That shows, no matter where they are,
When they can find excuse for grief.
If Gregory* be worth belief
(And every writer tells us so),
In some degree he lets us know
The reason for a prelacy
That has not God in company:
For all men's works, as they are founded
So shall they stand or be confounded;   290
He only that for love of Christ
Is eager to be beneficed –
And not for love of place, or pride
That prelates' names are dignified –
By reason, he will best endow
The Church, by virtue of that vow
With which his conscience has been bound;
But many clerks are to be found
So worldly-minded, they are glad
When holy orders may be had –   300
Not for the virtues of that state,
But only to grow rich and great
And be forever clear of need.
And thus, by pomp and petty greed,
Up go the Scribe and Pharisee
To Moses' or to Peter's See,
And sit aloft in that high chair,
And often damage, being there,
The faith entrusted to their keeping –
For Christ's cause finds them all day sleeping; 310
But worldly matters, wide awake.
Happy the man if he can take
Court-office, privileged and powered!
The trusty cash-box has devoured
(And thrown the key to Avarice)
The treasures of the benefice,

* The reference here is to the *Regula pastoralis.*

23

That do not feed, clothe, house, the poor –
Which is what they were given for.
Love walks a stranger, and unknown;
There is no grain of pity sown
By them; Sloth keeps the library
Assembled in the sanctuary.
For now such people need no more
Than to be wise in worldly lore.
Rich-Fare indulges his sweet tooth
So far that it destroys, in truth,
What little abstinence there is.
More closely to consider this,
In clerks are Etna's bonfires lit –
And all men are aware of it,
For Avignon's* experience
Has given them the evidence
Of how the Church may be divided.
And still the case is undecided,
Though it was written once for all
'Between two stools a man will fall
When most he thinks it safe to sit.'

But oh, to see the Church so split
Should cover all of us with gloom.
God grant him victory in whom
There is more truth and righteousness!
Yet it is seen that idleness,
When folk have handed round the cup,
Does harm when fiery blood is up,
If no one puts the bonfire out.
Consider now the latest sprout
Which pride and envy have made grow
From schism, and to which we owe
This recent sect of Lollardy,
And also many a heresy,

320

330

340

350

* The so-called 'Avignon Captivity', during which rival popes ruled simultaneously at Rome and at Avignon.

Among the very clerks themselves.
Better be one who digs and delves
And never in his faith has erred,
Than know the Bible word for word
And still go wrong, as some clerks do.
Upon one's hand to wear a shoe,
Or set one's gloves upon one's feet,
Is conduct neither wise nor meet
For men of reason to pursue:
If men held virtues in their view,   360
Such as Christ taught when here below,
We should see fewer of them go
About and be accounted wise,
While severally they disguise
The papacy beneath elections
That stick upon the predilections
Of various countries all about.
But when God wills, it shall wear out;
For truth must triumph at the last.
And yet they argue still so fast,   370
About the Pope and his estate,
They fall into extreme debate.
One clerk says Yea, another Nay;
And thus they spend the light of day,
And thus while each of them designs
His worldly increase, none inclines
To common profit: they declare
That God alone has power there,
To manifest His own intent.
They use no other argument   380
On points that threaten all belief –
Their one and only heartfelt brief,
To keep their world in their own claws;
As for the greater, common cause,
Not one of them will undertake,
Even for Holy Church's sake,
To hold a brief in its defence.

No help for truth and innocence,
But 'What I have, to that I hold'.

390 Lo, shattered thus is Jesus' fold;
His flock, abandoned by their guide,
Is eaten up both far and wide,
From lack of any pastoral care
By shepherds with no thought to spare
For any but their nearest kin.
The goad, instead of medicine,
They now employ; that heel is bruised
Whereon the ointment should be used;
And any wether thick in wool
400 They throw upon his back, and pull
And tease until they pluck him bare.
And though no other cause be there
But only their desire for gain,
Once started they will not restrain
Themselves, but let the act proceed;
And that is no good shepherd's deed.
This also has been told to me,
That from the level open lea
Into the briars they will force
410 Their flock, and by this cruel course
They hope to gain: by briars torn,
Some wool is left on every thorn;
And this they mark their own, by theft;
And thus the sheep are all bereft
And torn, from what their shepherds seize.
See how they palm off chalk for cheese!
For ably though they talk and teach,
They do not practise what they preach;
For if the hungry wolves appear,
420 That ghostly staff is nowhere near,
Wherewith the flock should be defended.
But if the poor sheep have offended,
No matter if their fault be light,

The rod is ready then to smite.
And thus, no matter what they say,
The beatings come the small man's way;
But as for the great men, they lack
The heart to beat a broader back;
Under the laws which clerks apply,
Our lot goes utterly awry.   430

I do not claim that all clerks are
Like this: some in particular
We find, in whom all virtue dwells;
And these, as the Apostle tells,
Are they who by Divine Election
Have been appointed to Perfection,
As Aaron was; and these we find
Are of a very different kind
From Simon Magus, who ignores
The fold-gate and seeks other doors;   440
For these go in the proper way.
But some there are, I have heard say,
Who follow close upon the heels
Of Simon and his cart, whose wheels
Are greediness and worldly pride;
And Holy Church walks at their side –
Showing upon its visage what,
Within its secret heart, is not.
For look at Holy Church, compare
What clergy do with what they swear: 450
There is no little difference.
They preach to us, their audience,
That no man shall his soul impair;
Earth's glory is a Cherry Fair
And nothing more, by what they tell.
Also they say there is a hell
Apt for the evils that men do;
They bid us therefore to eschew
All wickedness, and choose the good.

460 A man might think, who understood
Their words, that they would do the same;
Yet, between earnestness and game,
The case is often otherwise.
With holy stories they advise
How meritorious is that deed
Of charity, to clothe and feed
The poorer people, and to share
One's worldly wealth; but splitting their
Possession, they do not think good.
470 Further they tell us that we should,
By penance and by abstinence,
Live chastely and in continence.
But, to speak frankly about that,
I know not how a form so fat,
With dainty foodstuffs for its keep,
And laid so tenderly to sleep,
In all else pampered utterly,
Should still preserve its chastity:
However, I must hold my tongue
480 For fear of saying something wrong.
Whatever be the truth of it,
I lend my ears but not my wit;
It is no business of mine:
May He who made the Moon to shine,
Our God of goodness and of might,
If there be reason, put things right.
Yet, whatsoever men impute,
Good sense and truth may thus refute:
The vices of the wicked should
490 Be no discredit to the good;
For every man must bear the weight
Of his own deeds; in the estate
Of clerks, the good must be commended,
And all the rest by God amended;
For they are to the people's eye
The mirrors to rule conduct by,

To guide, and carefully to span
The distance between God and Man.

To speak now of the Third Estate:
It is a dreadful thing, the fate   500
That has befallen many lands!
How often, lacking hoops or bands,
A cask will suddenly surprise
By bursting when its ferments rise,
And let that liquor flood about
Which otherwise had not run out;
And often, too, a little chink
In an embankment, ere men think,
Lets in the stream – which with great pain,
If ever, they shall stem again.   510
He is not wise who does not know
That where laws are not, errors grow;
That was well-proved in days gone by.
This also is the common cry
In every land where people dwell:
All of them, in their mourning, tell
How the whole world has gone amiss;
Their judgements all agree on this,
Though they are differently stated.
But were there men who contemplated   520
Their true selves, and did not misuse
Their conscience, could they well accuse
Their God, Who always is the same?
Never, for in Him is no blame.
The fault, then, must be in ourselves –
And not by merely tens or twelves,
But totally, within us all:
Man is the cause that ills befall.

In some men's writings, all the same,
We read that Fortune is to blame;   530
And others are of the opinion
That starry patterns hold dominion

29

Over whatever men shall do;
And God knows which of them is true.
The world, by nature and by kind,
Was never to trust, in judgement blind,
And fallible in assigning fame:
It blames where there is naught to blame,
And praises what deserves no praise:
540 And thus whatever the world weighs,
There is deception in the scales.
And all the variance that prevails
Is ours, who ought to be more wise:
Exactly as we fall and rise,
So does the world arise and fall;
And thus mankind is all-in-all
The cause of its own weal and woe.
That which we call our fate, we owe
Ourselves alone; it springs from us.
550 If any man be dubious,
Then let him look at Israël:
Still while its people acted well,
Their fortune wore a smiling face;
But when they turned away from grace,
Their fortune too turned contrary.
And this proves well, and finally,
Why such amazement fills the earth,
And fullness always turns to dearth,
Though it seems thriving and at ease:
560 All things on earth are vanities,
And all mankind remains in doubt;
For the wheel turns and turns about,
Not for an hour is Fortune still;
No man alive has all his will.
Nothing, as far as we may know,
Endures beyond a breath or so;
The world stands ever in debate,
And safety dwells with no estate,
For here and there this world must go,

And up and down, and to and fro,   570
And ever has done and shall do.
There is a tale (which must be true,
For in the Book of Daniel
I find it) suiting this theme well.
To summarize its argument,
It shows that discord and dissent
Are why all earthly things decay,
And shall do till the Judgement Day;
That since the earliest Kingdom known,
If it has chanced, as in our own,   580
That change and revolution came,
Then Man himself must bear the blame –
Man by whose own ill governance
Arrives all earthly luck or chance.

[*There follows an almost word-for-word versification of that
part of the Book of Daniel (ii: 19–45) which deals with
Nebuchadnezzar's dream. Daniel interprets this dream as an
allegory of the progressive deterioration of the world. Gower
now turns to history for proof of that interpretation.*]

The World of Gold, the first of all,   670
Was in the lifetime of that King,
And it was long and flourishing;
And in those parts there was no nation
That Babylon, by subjugation,
Held not within its monarchy;
All rested in tranquillity
Until the days of change began:
And then the King of all Iran,
Cyrus by name, marched with his son
Cambyses against Babylon,   680
And broke its peace, and what they would
They did, and into servitude
They brought that Empire when at last
It had been captured and held fast.

Then was the King Belshazzar slain;
His all had vanished with his reign.
And thus when Babylon was won
The World of Silver had begun
And that of gold has passed away.
690 And thus it stood until the day
Of King Darius, in whose reign
The Persian empire changed again;
For Alexander, who had fought
Many amazing battles, brought
It low; so that the monarchy
Passed to the Greeks, and they rode high;
Persians were trodden down in dust,
For so men suffer who needs must.
Thus did the World of Silver pass,
700 And so began the World of Brass,
And for a little while advanced;
But then towards the end it chanced
The King had come to his last hour
And lay defeated by death's power.
He planned, however, to divide
His empire up, before he died,
Among the captains who had served
With him; to each, as each deserved,
He gave the kingdoms he had won.
710 Thereby were bitter wars begun
Among those men who were his heirs,
Such jealousy and pride were theirs;
Till fortune turned against them thus:
That noble Caesar, Julius,
Who then ruled all the Roman Land,
With mighty war and iron hand
All Persia, Greece, and the Chaldees
Won and subdued; so that, with these,
Not only all the Orient,
720 But marches of the Occident,
Bowed to his empire and his sword –

He, their unrivalled overlord,
Who held, what force of arms had won,
All earth as his dominion;
The first so worthy that he wore
The honoured name of Emperor.

Whomever Rome might then attack,
No power on earth could drive her back,
And every country must obey:
The World of Brass had passed away   730
And given place to that of steel,
Which now rode high on Fortune's wheel.
As, among metals, we shall find
Steel is by far the hardest kind,
So Rome was then the mightiest nation –
And long persisted in that station
Among the folk of Italy;
Till she turned so to villainy
That Leo, Emperor malign
As ever his son Constantine,*   740
Stole from the Holy Papacy
The patrimonial charity
Which that first Constantine, the Great,
To Pope Sylvester did donate.
Now Adrian sat in Peter's Chair,
And knew the harm of this affair;
To France he turns, there to complain
And to appeal to Charlemagne
For his soul's health to undertake
This quarrel, and for Jesus' sake   750
Stand by the Church as its defence.
And Charlemagne, in reverence
For God, took up the quarrel then,
And marched, with an array of men,

* Gower's history goes wildly astray in the whole of this passage
until l. 790. But since his drift is clear, there is perhaps no point in
correcting the details.

Over the hills of Lombardy;
And all the Roman tyranny
With sword and blood was overthrown:
By strength he made the town his own;
And, once in power, such feats he wrought
760 That Holy Church once more was brought
To freedom, and he could restore
Sylvester's loss, and give him more.
And thus when Charlemagne had served
His God, he took – and well deserved –
The diadem, as Emperor
By coronation: nevermore
Did any Roman wear the crown
Or rule the Empire from that town;
But many years men saw it stand
770 Beneath the Frankish king's command,
Until the Wheel of Fortune's roll
Gave it for Lombards to control –
Not by the sword, by sufferance
Of him who then was King of France.
Carolus Calvus* was his name,
And it was he resigned his claim,
And let the Roman Empire go
To Louis, his Lombard cousin. So
It lasted till the fatal year
780 Of Albert and of Berenger;
But then it chanced they disagreed,
And that the friendships would not speed
Between those two that were so great;
And so they lost their whole estate,
Honour and earthly happiness.
Proverbially, none the less,
Men say how rare it is that Wealth
Can bear to see an equal's health;
And in the mutual strife between
790 The Lombards, this was clearly seen:

* Charles II (the Bald), 840–77.

Such were their envy and their greed
That all men with a troop to lead
Would drag their partisans about
Within the City and without.
The common rights no champion saw,
So that all government of law
Was lost by them; and, sure as Fate,
By reason that they reached that state
Only because they would contend,
They found it needful in the end   800
To ask for foreign intervention.

And thus, because of this dissension,
And all the empire gone awry,
Seven princes out of Germany
Were chosen, and with this provision:
On their electoral decision
The empiry of Rome should stand.
And thus what slipped the Lombard's hand,
For want of grace, and was forsaken,
The Germans now have undertaken: 810
And, to make sure of their estate,
All that they found in such debate
They took to their own government,
And by unanimous assent
Among themselves; and thereupon
They set a German on the throne
(Chronicles tell us that his name
Was Otto). It has been the same
Ever since that day until this:
The Roman Empire was and is   820
In German hands. And in this wise
(As you have heard me analyse
The dream that Daniel expounded,
The image upon which he founded
All the world's future and its fall),
Ours is the latest age of all.

This world now stands upon the feet
Of earth and steel, and in complete
Disunion – which began to grow
830   When Rome fell into discord so:
And truly, that is to deplore;
For ever since, and more and more,
The world is worsened every day.
To show the truth of this, we may
Find Rome the best place to begin:
The city walls and all within
Are ruined now, and overthrown;
The town lies waste; green fields have grown
Where once the Palace was. And more:
840   If we consider what, before,
The Romans were, and in what heights
With all their citizens and knights,
And weigh them against what remain,
Then they are chaff compared with grain.
And where is all the Roman might?
Now almost nothing stands upright,
Of honour or of worldly good,
As in the early days it stood.
And why has honour fled away?
850   A man might answer, truth to say,
That the whole cause was dissidence,
From which confusion will commence,
As from a mother, everywhere –
Not only in a Church affair,
But in a temporal matter too.
Experience tells us this is true,
And has done, many a day ere this,
Through worldly things whose poison is
Now mingled with the Church's blood:
860   For Christ Himself makes understood
That no man may together serve
God and this world, unless he swerve
Between the two, and be unstable;

36

And Christ's word cannot be a fable.
So plain it is to every eye,
There is no need to clarify
This matter, or say more of it;
But it informs a man of wit
How this our world has come about,
And how it is well-nigh worn out,   870
According to that allegory
Which Daniel, in the Bible story,
Expounded, as you have been told.
The Brass, the Silver, and the Gold,
All of these worlds have passed away;
On ancient feet of brittle clay
And iron stands the world we see;
And clay and iron disagree.
So that it needs must swerve and swing,
Like every ill-compounded thing.   880

The Apostle writes for one and all,
And says that upon us will fall
The world's end; and by this we know
We are near that statue's overthrow
By which this world was signified:
Once it was great and glorified,
And now is feeble, old, and vile,
And full of peril and of guile,
And its components are discrete
Just as we saw the statue's feet   890
Were, that I have described above.
And this men see: when lack of love
Causes dissension in the land,
Prosperity can never stand.
And nowadays, on every side,
A man may see the world divide;
Such universal wars have come
Among the folk of Christendom,
That after vengeance all men reach;

37

900 And yet the clergy always preach
That no good deed can ever be
That is not based on charity.
I ask how charity may stand
With deadly wars on every hand.
But Man is cause of all these woes;
Wisdom he has, reason he knows;
Whereof a sign and witness is,
The statue's lineaments were his
And not some other creature's; for
910 Man was ordained as governor,
At first, of every creature made
(But afterwards his power decayed):
When Adam fell, the beasts too fell;
When he was ill, they were not well;
For as a man may suffer through
His sickness, other creatures too
Will suffer in comparison.
Those heavenly forms, the Moon and Sun,
First with man's sin becoming wroth,
920 See how eclipses hide them both!
By sin the purest air aloft
Has been, and is, corrupted oft;
For now we feel the storm-winds blow,
Yet the next moment they sink low;
Now cloudy weather, and now clear:
Plainly from this it may appear
That human sin is to abhor,
Which drives the very skies to war.
And if we summon to our mind
930 The qualities of every kind
Of thing among us here below,
All of them ever vary so:
Now the sea ebbs and now it flows;
Now the field withers, now it grows;
Now every tree has leaves of green,
Now they are bare and none are seen;

Now spring the lovely summer flowers,
Now fall the stormy winter showers;
And every day gives way to night;
Nothing that stands unchanged, upright: 940
Now there is sunlight, and now murk;
And thus goes all our earthly work,
According to the disposition
Of man, and to mankind's condition.
And therefore Gregory,* in his
Moralia, says that each man is
A little world made cunningly;
And this he proves quite readily:
In that man's soul is rational,
His nature is angelical;   950
Five senses, like a beast, has he;
And he is growing like a tree;
And has mere being, like a stone.
And thus a man is, of his own
Nature, as learned authors say,
A microcosm in his way;
And if the Little World should run
Awry, the Greater is undone.
The land, the sea, the circling heaven,
All ask for judgement to be given   960
Against mankind, and war on him:
For while man's hinge hangs out of trim,
All other things will be askew.
And thus – I set it down as true –
Man is the reason of all woe,
And why this world is troubled so.

Disunion, the Gospel shows,
Will make one family oppose
Another, till the realm be wrecked.
Plain, then, to every intellect   970
It is: disunion before all

* The reference is to *Moralia*, vi: 16.

Other things, makes the world to fall –
And has done, since the world began.
The finest proof of this is Man;
For men being, in their temperaments,
Made of conflicting elements* –
The cold, the hot, the moist, the dry –
Their very nature is to die:
There is such war in their complexion,
980   Between each humour and affection,
That, until one part be repressed,
No final peace is for the rest.
But were Man otherwise, made all
Of only one material,
Entire and without interruption,
Then there could never be corruption
Engendered in that unity;
But since there is diversity
Within him, he may not endure,
990   And in the end his death is sure.
And further, in a man there is
Yet more diversity than this,
Which keeps him in continual strife
As long as he has any life:
The body and the soul also
Are diverse, and each other's foe;
So that those things the soul abhors
The body fights for, and adores.
And yet in all this war between
1000   These two, it is not seldom seen
The battle is not to the strong.
Search but your memory, among
The world's events, both old and new:
Is not this warfare much to rue,
That first began in Paradise?

* This (l. 976 ff.) is the Aristotelian doctrine that all things, living
or not, are compounded of various mixtures of the primal 'ele-
ments' – air, fire, water, and earth. See Book Seven, l. 203 ff., p. 234.

40

For there it showed, without disguise,
Its nature, and what grief it wrought;
Out of that warfare there were brought
Forth vice and every deadly sin,
Through which disunion came in   1010
On earth among humanity,
And was the cause and reason why
God called the mighty floods to birth
And made an end of all the earth
Save Noah and his company,
Whose ship gave them security.
Also by sin it came about
That Nimrod grew so bold and stout
That he built up the towering height
Of Babel – as if he would fight   1020
Against the power of God on high;
Confounded in that hour thereby
Were languages, to such intent
That no man knew what others meant,
So that the work could not proceed.
And thus it is with every deed
Or enterprise with sin allied:
Its power will not long abide;
For, by its very quality,
Sin must bring forth discordancy,   1030
Betokening when this world shall wane.
For verily, as Christ makes plain,
A little ere the world's decay
Concord and peace shall pass away,
And loving-kindness too shall cease
Among mankind, and hate increase;
And when these tokens have been shown,
Then suddenly shall fall the stone,
As Daniel has let us know,
Which all this world shall overthrow;   1040
And then shall all the dead arise
Either to joy or to assize,

41

And go where they shall always dwell,
Swiftly to heaven or to hell.
In heaven is peace and harmony;
All hell is such disunity,
No love-day dawns among them there.
Best, then, while there is time to spare,
To make our peace one with another
1050   And love our neighbour like our brother;
So may we gather worldly wealth
And, later, spiritual health.

But would to God one man there were
Now, with Arion to compare,
Whose harp contained such harmony
(And to it so melodiously
He sang), that not a beast so wild
But his tune made it tame and mild:
The lion warred not with the hind;
1060   To sheep the ravening wolf was kind,
The hound lay quiet with the hare;
And every person everywhere
Who heard Arion's harmonies –
Master and man alike – all these
Were bound by him in kind accord;
The commoner towards his lord,
And lords to commons equally,
He led in peace and amity,
And drove away all sadnesses.
1070   That was a merry tune of his,
When every man laughed with his brother:
And were there now but such another
To harp as he did, who is dead,
Oft might he stand us in good stead
By making peace where there was hate;
For on the threshold of debate
No better guardian can be had.
But where all wisdom has run mad,

And reason turns to savageness,
And all restraint becomes excess   1080
Throughout the world, then dread is here;
For that brings in the general fear
Which lurks at everybody's door:
But when the horse's side is sore
Where the sharp spur struck home and tore,
Is frequent grief.
     And now no more
About this subject shall be said,
Which may by God alone be sped.

Good were it, therefore, at this tide,   1090
If every man on every side
Were to beseech and pray for peace,
Which is the cause of all increase
In honour and in worldly wealth,
Heart's rest, and spiritual health.
Where peace is not, is nothing good:
Therefore, to Christ Who shed His blood
For peace, pray now, all mortal men.
Amen. Amen. Amen. Amen.

Book One: Pride

I MAY not stretch up to the heavens
This hand of mine, nor set at evens
This world that wavers on the scales:
Little my slender power avails
To compass things so great and high;
So I must let them pass me by,
And find new matters to recite.
Therefore the style of what I write,
From this day forth I mean to change,
And treat of what is not so strange –
Something that every creature learns,
And whereupon the whole world turns
And so has turned since it began,
And shall while yet there is a man:
And it is Love of which I mean
To treat, as shortly shall be seen.
In love, men lose their self-command,
For love will come to no one's hand;
Thus almost all men must admit
Too little or too much of it;
Moreover there is not a man
Alive who is so wise, he can
Set it in tune and temperance,
Unless it comes about by chance:
For help is none, in strength or skill;
And he whom boasting else would fill,
Is soonest levelled with the ground,
And nowhere may a cure be found.
For never yet was secret art
Which had a medicine to impart
Against what God by natural
Law has decreed; among us all,

None knows the salve for such a sore.
Love was, and is, and evermore
Shall be our master where he will,
In spite of all our mortal skill;
For wheresoever he wills to stay,
There is no power to say him nay.
But what shall come about at last,
No wit may certainly forecast,   40
Save that pure chance may draw the veil;
For if there ever were a scale
Whose balance is by Fate controlled,
Well may I trust what I am told,
And what no skill may understand:
The scales are tilted by Love's hand.
For Love is blind and cannot see,
And so there is no certainty
To set on his arbitrament,
But, with the turning wheel's intent,   50
He gives his graces undeserved;
Often, from people who have served
Him well, he takes all benefice,
As from a man who plays at dice
And cannot know his luck at all
Until he sees how they will fall
And make him either lose or win.
Many a time will men begin
An enterprise they would amend
If they could see how it would end.   60

As proof that this is verity,
Myself am in that company
And School, a full licentiate.
The time ago is not so great
(While we are on the subject, you
Shall hear, if you are willing to),
That I endured a wondrous thing,
Severe and full of suffering,

Which had to do with love and fate;
70 This I would fain communicate,
Fully and plainly to speak out.
To all you lovers round about
I shall in detail now declare,
In writing, all my woeful care,
My woeful day, my woeful lot,
So that you shall remember what
Hereafter comes before your eyes:
For in good faith I would advise
You, take example while you may
80 Of wisdom when it comes your way,
That by good teaching you consign
The truth abroad: such a design
Is praiseworthy. So I propose,
Plainly, in writing, to disclose
How love and I together met –
Whereby the world which is not yet
May take example, when I go,
From that unhappy pleasing woe
Whose government has gone astray
90 (Now joy, and now joy-fled-away),
Yet there is no withstanding it
By any force of human wit.

Now of this matter that befell,
Concerning love, and me as well,
I mean to make the details clear;
Read on, then, if you wish to hear
How fate would have it that I fared.
And first of all, be this declared:
As I walked out the other day,
100 It being then the month of May
When every bird upon the Earth
Has found his mate, and sings in mirth
For love that loves again, then I
Was nowise comforted thereby;

For I was farther from my love
Than Earth is from the Heavens above;
Nor any hope that I could see.
No better counsel came to me:
Like one worn out with journeying,
I sought the woods, but not to sing   110
Among the birds; for when I found
Myself at the woods' heart, a ground
Of pleasant level green arose;
There I lamented in my woes,
Wishing and weeping all alone;
And other music made I none.
So bitter to me was this pain
That I was dashed to earth again
And yet again, and had no breath;
And all the while, I longed for death.   120
Then, when I woke from out my grief,
I prayed to heaven for relief,
With many a piteous look above:
'Goddess of Love, and God of Love –
Thou, Venus; Cupid, thou her son –
Whither are pity and mercy gone?
Now let me wholly live or die;
For such a malady as I
Now have and, truly, long have had,
Might cause a Magus to run mad   130
If it should overlong endure.
O Venus, Queen of passion's cure,
Men's life, men's joy, thou balm of need;
Take notice of the cause I plead;
Yield me a little of thy grace;
Resolve me in this very place
If thou hast any grace at all.'
And as I let my words down fall,
I saw the God and Goddess both.
But he, the King of Love, turned wroth   140
Eyes on me, and askance looks cast,

And moved away from me at last.
And yet it seemed, before he went,
He took a fiery dart and sent
It through my deepest heart: be sure
I found in him no other cure;
He had no mind for lingering.
But she, who is the Well and Spring
(For them that love) of joy or pain,
150   Chose at that season to remain.
But I must set down here that she
Turned no kind countenance on me,
Though none the less she said: 'Who art
Thou, son?' With that I gave a start,
Like men awakened suddenly;
And this she noted, bidding me
Put from my mind all thought of fear.
And even so, I felt no cheer,
For I could see no reason why.
160   Once more she asked me who was I.
I said: 'A wretch who lieth here:
What is your will, my Lady dear?
Am I to heal or perish?' She
Said: 'Son, what is thy malady,
The hurt of which thou so complainest?
Conceal it not, for if thou feignest,
I cannot medicine to thee.'
'Madame, I wear your livery,
And long within your Courts have served;
170   I ask for what I have deserved,
Comfort in place of my long woe.'
With that she drew her eyebrows low,
And said: 'There are too many of you
Pretenders: if so be thou too
Pretendest, and be such a one,
Count well the service thou hast done.'
And this she said though knowing well
My wheel of fortune stood or fell

Without the touch of counterfeit.
She bade me none the less repeat   180
What ailed me, and to speak the truth.
'Madame, if you showed any ruth,'
I said, 'then I would answer you.'
'Disclose thy sickness through and through;
Speak on, and say how it befell.'
'And that, Madame, I can do well,
If I but live so long.' Then she
Again looked frowningly at me.
'In case thou livest, my command
Is first that thou be shriven. And,   190
For all that I myself well know
How it is with thee, even so
I will that thou confessest all
Thy thoughts and deeds, both great and small,
Unto my priest, who will appear.
My Chaplain, Genius, be here
To shrive this man!'
                    When this was said,
At once I lifted up my head,
And there beheld him as he came –
That priest whom she had called by name.   200
He sat down, ready to confess me;
And, first of all, began to bless me.

This worthy priest, this holy man,
Addressed me, and he thus began:
'Now, my son, say I *benedicite*;
I tell thee that of all felicity,
And of all woe, that love has given
To thee, thou shalt this day be shriven.
What love has caused thee, before this,
To suffer, tell, and nothing miss;   210
As all occurred to thee, tell all.'
And at these words, down did I fall
Upon my knees; and with devotion,

And with a most contrite emotion,
I said, '*O Sancte Domine*,
O Father Genius, shriving me,
Because thou hast experience
Of Love, for whom in reverence
I am to be confessed today,
I beg thee let me not miss-say
My shrift – for I am so disturbed
Throughout my heart, and so perturbed,
And all my senses so upset,
That there is much I shall forget:
But if thou question all, and sift
Every detail of my shrift,
Nothing, I think, will be omitted;
But now I am so dimly witted,
I trust not my self-mastery.'
Then he began to preach to me:
Gentle and courteous his words were,
And thus he spoke me, soft and fair:
'To shrive you here, and question you,
My son, I was assigned to do
By Venus, goddess from above,
Whose priest I am, concerning love.
But there are certain reasons, still,
Why I both must and ever will
In my discourse not only tell
Of love, but other things as well
To which the vices may relate;
For this is proper to that state
Of priesthood to whose order I
Belong. I shall pass nothing by
Till I have shown, omitting none,
All vices to you, one by one:
After which proof you may decide
To take your conscience as your guide.
And yet my plan is finally
To try, and judge, especially

In love, as one who serves the same –
Which is the reason why I came.
Both things, then, I propose for you:
First, that which is my Order's due,
To set the vices all a-row;
But next, above all else, to show
What are love's signs and properties,
Ranked by their orders and degrees
According to the governance
Of Venus, she whose ordinance   260
I must obey, who am constrained.
For being so by love retained,
I am the less to blame although
There is not very much I know
Of other kinds of wisdom: I
Learned not in their academy:
I have not, in the general way,
On vice and virtue, much to say;
Only of love and of love's lore;
Because in Venus' books no more,   270
In either gloss or text, is taught.
But inasmuch as, to my thought,
Good manners will a priest enhance,
While he is shamed by ignorance,
With all the forms of priesthood I
Shall guide thy shrift so teachingly
That at the least thou shalt have learned
The vices, which I shall have turned
So towards your loving purposes,
You shall know what each means and is,   280
Since all a man may say or hear
In his confession, must be clear:
No need for curious art or grace;
Truth does not wear a painted face:
Therefore all that I ask shall be,
My son, so clearly put to thee,
That thou shalt hear and comprehend.

The points on which all shrifts depend.'

Held between life and death I heard
290   This chaplain out, and said no word;
But then I begged that he would say
His will, and promised to obey,
In every detail, his decree;
And this is how he answered me:
He bade me first that I should shrive
All that concerned my senses five,
And make provision for correction
Of any waste or misdirection.

CONFESSOR:

For each is properly a door
300   Into the heart, and evermore
Through them come thronging to the fair
Those many things that may impair
Man's soul. And now that I have brought
This point up, first, my son, my thought
Is to inquire about your sight –
Which is, if I am taught aright,
The most important sense of all
Through which some peril may befall.

And if we speak with love in mind,
310   How many folk are of the kind
Which goes about with roving eye
Forever trying to espy
Things which are often no concern
Of theirs, except that their hearts turn
To grudging other folk their right;
And thus full many a worthy knight,
And many a lovesome lady, both,
Have oft had cause for being wroth.
Think, then, the eye is like a thief
320   Of love, that brings both harm and grief;

And furthermore, for its own part,
Full many a time that fiery dart
Of love, whose burning never dies,
Transfixes hearts by way of eyes:
Thus, often, sight may be the first
To grieve a man, and grieve him worst,
And many a time himself may know
That thence his own misfortunes grow.
Therefore, hear now a tale whereby
Thou mayst learn caution of the eye,   330
My son, and keep close guard on it
Lest it attempt what is unfit.

Ovid informs us, in his book,*
Of one case of a sinful look:
Long since, there lived a knight of fame
And worth – Actaeon was his name –
A nephew to that Cadmus, King
Of Thebes, who was the first to bring
That city to its power and height.
Actaeon thought, as well he might,   340
He had no rival and no peer;
His habit was, from year to year,
To go with hounds and mighty horns
Among the forests and the thorns,
To seek what he might hunt or chase:
And where he pleased, in any place
Where game perchance might cross his way,
There he would ride to hunt and play.
It happened one day that as he
Rode out upon his venery,   350
Alone in the deep woods he was.
And there among the long green grass
He saw the fair fresh flowers spring,
Heard in the leafy branches sing
The throstle and the nightingale,

* *Metamorphoses*, Book Three.

And so unthinking reached a dale –
A little space of level ground
Full of green bushes all around
Most thickly grown, and cedars high.
360   Within it then he cast his eye:
Amid the clearing was a well
More beautiful than tongue can tell;
And there Diana naked stood
And bathed and sported in the flood,
With many a nymph to minister.
He could not look away from her
And from her utter nakedness.
But she grew angry to excess;
And, as a goddess, having power,
370   She changed his form upon the hour
Into the likeness of a hart's.
Up then before his hounds he starts,
Where they run busily about
With many a horn-call in the rout;
And loudly after him they cry.
So in the end, most wretchedly,
By his own vengeful hounds this hart
Was slaughtered and then torn apart.

Think now, my son, what it can mean
380   If men see what should not be seen;
Actaeon learned it to his pain;
Be wary, therefore, and refrain.
For heedful men would oft agree,
To wink is better than to see.

[*To prove this, the Confessor cites another story from Ovid –
that of Perseus and the Gorgons* (Metamorphoses, *Book
Four, 772 ff.*). *Gower confuses them, however, with the Graiae.
Since Boccaccio also does this, it is possible that he, not Ovid,
was Gower's direct authority for the story. The Confessor's
moral is obvious.*]

CONFESSOR:

Therefore, my son, be circumspect,
That thou shalt use thine eyes aright;
Let not Medusa catch thy sight,
Lest thou be turned into a stone:
No man so wise was ever known,   440
Unless he guarded well his sight
And gave no heed to vain delight,
But was by pleasure often caught,
And by the strength of love made naught.
Now I have told, and thou hast heard,
What happens when the eye has erred;
Good my son, heed it well therefore.
I would advise thee, what is more,
That of thine hearing thou beware,
For that into the heart may bear   450
Tidings of many vanities
Which fill men's thought with dire disease.
Good, even so, that men should turn
Their ears to things from which they learn
That which to virtue appertains;
But, from whatever else remains,
Better to turn one's ear away;
Else, if men do not so, they may
Full often be unfortunate.
Let one example indicate   460
How men do well to be in fear
Lest they are careless what they hear.

There is a serpent, Aspidis*
By name, whose property is this:
The carbuncle, which people call

* This legend is derived from Psalm lviii, 4: '... the deaf adder
that stoppeth her ear'. The ingenious method of doing so may be
found in St Augustine. The carbuncle in the adder's head was
probably suggested by the legendary jewel in the head of the toad.

The noblest gem-stone of them all,
It wears high up within its head;
And when a cunning man is led
To want the stone, and tame the snake
470 By singing cantrips he will make,
When Aspidis begins to hear,
He lies down flat upon his ear,
Close to the ground, and stops it tight;
The other ear, with all his might,
He closes with his tail – so well
That not a word of all the spell,
That should enchant him, stirs his sense;
Such is the serpent's self-defence,
By means of which he turns away
480 Words that might lead his ear astray.

[*This point is illustrated by the story of how Ulysses stopped the ears of his crew, so that they should not be led astray by the Sirens.*]

CONFESSOR:

530 My son, this lesson were most meet
To be remembered now and here;
For, as I say, of all your ear
Receives, beware; believe it not,
Unless more evidence be got.
And if thou wishest to beware
And wisely learn the guard and care
Of eye and ear, I advocate
Again that thou must close the gate
On folly such as will unknit
540 Thy inward spiritual wit,
And whereof now thy love exceeds
All measure, and much sorrow breeds.
But if these two are ruled by thee,
How easy then to rule the three:
And therefore I forbear to shrive

Thee further, of thy senses five,
But now speak only of these two.
Tell me, then, first, if it be true
That thou hast used thine eyes amiss.

GOWER:

Yes, father, I confess to this;   550
Medusa they have seen indeed,
And I have no excuse to plead:
And now my heart is turned to stone,
And thus my lady thereupon
Love's image has so deep-engraved
That I am powerless to be saved.

CONFESSOR:

What sayst thou, son, about thine ear?

GOWER:

There, father, too, my guilt is clear.
When I may listen to my love,
All rudderless my senses rove: 560
Ulysses did as I do not;
I fall at once upon the spot
Wherein I see my lady stand;
And there, as you must understand,
I am so troubled in my thought
That all my reason is distraught,
By which I should have been defended.

CONFESSOR:

By God, good son, be thou amended:
For it would seem, to hear thee speak,
Thy wits are very far to seek.   570
I have no further points to cite
About thy hearing and thy sight;
But into other matters I
Must ask, to see how they may lie.

My son, I now have to report
That there are of another sort
Of deadly vices seven defined –
Whereby the heart is oft inclined
To things which later cause it grief.
580 Of these, the first sin and the chief
Is Pride: he is the master, and
He has with him at his command
Five servants of the most diverse,
Whose names I purpose to rehearse.
The first is called Hypocrisy:
If thou art of his company,
Tell all, my son, and shrive thee clean.

GOWER:

Father, I know not what you mean.
But there is one thing I would pray
590 Of you: inform me, in some way,
What constitutes a hypocrite;
Then, if I am to blame in it,
I will confess what is amiss.

CONFESSOR:

My son, a hypocrite is this:
A man all feigning and pretence
Of purity and innocence
Without, who is not so within;
One who does this with mind to win
The vain reward of his ambition.
600 And when he comes to that position,
Reveals what all the time he was:
And then the wheat is turned to grass;
And where the rose grew, lies a thorn;
And he who seemed a lamb is shorn
Into a wolf – for evil so
Lies hidden underneath a show
Of righteousness; and, rumour tells,

The Orders* all know where he dwells,
Who is their privy counsellor;
And all that world which they before   610
Relinquished, he brings back again.
He will clothe riches, folk maintain
In the plain weeds of poverty;
And does, to stand out worthily,
Deeds inwardly of little price.
In public he says 'Fie!' to vice;
In private, nothing so perverse
But he is found to be its nurse;
And ever his looks are douce and soft,
And where he goes he blesses oft,   620
And thus the blind world is misled.
Nor does he rest when he has spread
His empire on the Orders: when
He has possessed that class of men
Among all such as claim to be
Of Holy Church, we find how he
Can work among the wide furred hoods
To make them rich in worldly goods.
And these men are the very same
Who most regard the world with blame;   630
Though, clean against their teaching, there
Is naught they would not sooner spare;
So, seeming all of light, they do
Deeds that are darkness through and through.
Thus insincere Hypocrisy,
With his apparent piety,
Has fixed a vizard on his face,
Whereby in terms of worldly grace
He seems to be a man of parts –
Yet bears the worst of cursèd hearts.   640
Nevertheless, he is believed,
And very often has achieved

* Monks and friars, as distinct from the rest of the clergy. 'He',
in this line, is Hypocrisy personified.

His longed-for honour and world's wealth –
And takes it, one might say, by stealth,
Under the cover of deceit.
And, in like manner, one shall meet
With men who hold this sin's commission
In many a secular position –
Yet only great men; of the small
650 He will take no account at all;
But those above the common sort,
With them he pleases to consort.
On folk whom he has sworn to aid,
He will not rest till he has preyed;
For nowadays is many a one
Who mouths of Peter and of John
But is Iscariot at heart.
No wordly treasure shall depart
His hands; yet he gives alms away,
660 Fasts often, goes to Mass, will say
His *mea culpa* (oft expressed),
And lay his hand upon his breast
And, therewith, upwards cast his eye
As if he saw Christ in the sky.
People might think, at the first sight,
That he, without assistance, might
Save all the world with holy prayer.
And yet his true heart is elsewhere
Than in his prayers, though most devout
670 They be; for worldly ends, about
It goes to seek how it may snatch
Advantages.
        And we may match
This among lovers of the sort
Who feign most humbly to comport
Themselves, but with hypocrisy;
One, by deceit and flattery,
Has cozened many a virtuous wife.
He whets his blarney like a knife;

60

Then, with soft words and pleasant lies,
And his assumed most-piteous guise,   680
He would make any woman sure
She walked a grassy plain, secure –
Whereas she stumbles in the mire.
For if he gains but his desire,
What aftermath may lie beyond
He finds not written in his bond.
But till his moment of success
There is no trick which, under stress,
Any false lover may have played,
But he will call it to his aid –   690
As is appropriate in his place.
He will use medicine till his face
Is coloured like the rainy moon;
Then he asks pity, and his boon,
For sickness, though all this is feigned.
With countenance thus marred and stained,
And gaze cast up to her, he sighs,
And changes face in many a wise
To bring his lady to believe
In what he wishes to achieve,   700
Explaining thus his ashen hue;
So, to convince her he is true,
He will seem sick when he is hale.
And yet, when lowest droops his sail,
Then is he swiftest to beguile
That woman who has all this while
Given him trust and confidence.

Son, if thou hast done violence
To thine own soul in such a way,
Then in thy shrift thou shalt survey   710
And tell me it, if it be so.

GOWER:

Indeed, my holy father, no.

I never have had need at all
To feign such sickness; for I call
Our God to witness, I have shown
Less sickness than my heart has known.
This also I may well avow:
So lowly I could never bow,
To show a feigned humility,
720   But all the heartfelt thoughts of me
Were longing to bow lowlier yet.
For one thing I shall never let
Slip from me towards my lady dear:
Not to be all that I appear.
God knows, I never lied in aught;
My look was mirror to my thought;
For – may my faith and truth be heeded –
My wish a thousand-fold exceeded
All I could show by looks or tongue.
730   But, sir, if ever I when young
Did otherwise, in any place,
For this I ask your pardoning grace.
I shall not plead in my defence
That but for this, in every sense,
Towards Love and all his company
I have used no hypocrisy;
But there is one – she whom I serve –
For whom, although I may deserve
No thanks from her, up till today
740   My speech is always Yea or Nay
According as my thoughts dictate.
For others, I will not debate
That I in some degree am fit
For blaming as a hypocrite.

CONFESSOR:

My son, in all men we require
Their word and honour kept entire
And pure, towards Love, in every way;

For if we carefully survey
What happens in this kind of case,
We shall assume no feigning face   750
To deal with love untruthfully.
Loving is all heart's liberty;
But if deceitfully thou feignest,
And thereby thy desire attainest,
All that which thou hast gained by guile –
Though it may please thee for a while –
Shall make thee afterwards repine.
To illustrate this point of mine,
The chronicles have tales that prove
The fate of those who cozen love.   760

[*The first of these tales is that of Mundus and Paulina, which
may be found in Josephus. At Rome there dwelt a beautiful and
virtuous lady named Paulina. A knight called Mundus bribed
the priests of Isis into cajoling her to spend a night in their
temple. Pretending to be the god Anubis, Mundus enjoyed her –
and afterwards boasted of it to her. She reported him, with the
result that the priests were put to death and their temple
desecrated, while Mundus was banished. There follows an
account of the Trojan Horse, based mainly upon Benoît de
Sainte-More's* Roman de Troie, *and upon Guido di Col-
onna's* Historia Troiana. *Although some details are Gower's
own, there is no great point in retelling the story here. The
Confessor again points the obvious moral:*]

CONFESSOR:

And thus fell out that treachery   1185
Which under false hypocrisy
Lay hid; and they who dreamed of peace
Could never win to a release
From that same all-devouring sword;
Thus many a savour, when explored,   1190
Turns sour, that had seemed sweet to taste:
He squanders many a word in waste,

Who has to do with folk like these;
For when gain most seems his to seize,
Then most he is in shape to lose.
And just so, if a woman choose
Some man because of what she hears
Him say, the truer he appears,
The less sincerity is his.

1200 Yet many a time – and pity it is –
Success is for the most untrue,
Who every morning love anew,
Whereby their love shall soon grow loth
And have good reason to be wroth.
But if a lover so desire
His pleasure that he shall conspire
And feign and lie for its achieving,
He may be certain of receiving
His punishment, as oft we see.

1210 Therefore, my son, I say to thee,
Thou shalt do well if thou tak'st care
By all thy manhood to forswear
Hypocrisy and counterfeit,
So that thou practise not deceit
And make a woman trust in what
Thou inwardly believest not;
For from such false hypocrisy
In love, springs all the treachery
By which love is deceived so oft;
1220 For a feigned manner is so soft,
Love cannot easily take care.
Therefore, my son, I will not spare
To charge thee, put that sin away,
That has made many a woman stray,
And meddle not with that affair.

GOWER:
Father, I will no more, I swear.

64

CONFESSOR:

My son, see that thou keep'st thy vow:
For all that thou hast heard till now
Has dealt with the first form of pride.
There is a second sort beside,   1230
Of the same vice; and now of this
To speak and shrive, I must not miss;
I promised thee, and now commence:
Its name is Disobedience.

This vice of disobedience stands
Against one's conscience's commands;
All that is meek, it disallows;
To God Himself it never bows,
Nor to His words of law, at all.
Like some inhuman animal   1240
In chase of pleasure, fierce and wild,
This proud sin scorns so to be mild
That every law but curls his lip;
He never knows true fellowship;
For pride, he will not serve, nor may.
Thus he is bad in every way,
The man of whom all men avow
That he will break but never bow.
I know not whether love might bend him;
What other power might amend him   1250
At heart, I cannot bring to mind.

So if thy heart has such a kind
Of disposition or of feeling,
Speak up, my son, without concealing;
For if thou art intransigent
Towards love, then to no great extent
May thy ambition be achieved.

GOWER:

My father, be it well believed,

65

The little pup whose master taught
1260   Him well, gives no more heed and thought
To lie when he is told 'Go low',
Than I, whenever I may know
My lady's will, bow down amain.
I sometimes bitterly complain,
Though, of some of my lady's acts;
And I shall tell you all the facts:
For in two points, as I conceive,
I could not, if I would, achieve
Obedience to her behest;
1270   There are no more – in all the rest
I may be bidden; only two;
And this I dare to promise you.

CONFESSOR:

What are those two? Tell on (*said he*).

GOWER:

My father, this is one: when she
Commands my lips no more to stir,
And that I cease to question her
In love (of which I often preach),
But to forbear that kind of speech
Outright, and let her be in peace,
1280   For all this world I could not cease;
I have no power to obey:
When I am with her, though she may
Forbid me to make speeches, still
I must go counter to her will,
To try if I may come to grace;
But this I never can embrace,
Whatever I may do or say.
Yet oft I speak in such a way
That she is wroth, and says 'Be still'.
1290   If that behest I should fulfil,
Because of such obedience

66

My hopes would be without defence –
No men succeed unless they speak.
I know not what advice to seek,
But certainly must disobey;
For I could never bear to say
Nothing at all of all I mean:
For it is always fresh and green,
The great love that I bear in me;
And so it is, I cannot be   1300
Both vocal and obedient:
Thus I am seldom reticent;
And this is the first point in which
My virtue is not up to pitch;
And yet it is not caused by pride.

And now there is the other side
Of my transgression to recount.
It causes me no small amount
Of grief, nor may I understand
Why oft my lady will command   1310
That I find someone else to woo,
And says that if I really knew
How distant from her grace I stood,
Then choose anew I surely would.
But here again I disobey;
For she might just as lightly say,
'Go pluck the moon from where it sits,'
As to set that before my wits;
For never yet a rooted tree
Stood firm and fast in such degree   1320
That I stand not more firm and fast
In loving her, and could not cast
My heart off even if I would.
For, God knows, though she never should
Stand in my sight after today,
Still it were true: there is no way
This passion from my breast to pull.

Such fealty is wonderful,
When – willy-nilly on her part –
1330 I bear her an unchanging heart.
What other is there I could choose?
No matter if I win or lose,
Still I must love her till I die.
And so at such times I defy
Her every order and behest;
But I obey in all the rest.
Therefore, my father, I beseech
You: formally, in full, now teach
Me all there is, if there is more,
1340 Pertaining to this kind of lore,
So that thereby I learn to rule
My heart according to Love's school.

CONFESSOR:

Of the dependants of this sin
There are two others, close akin;
Their names are Murmur and Complaint;
And no man has the skill to paint
Their face with hues of happiness:
For though good luck brings them success,
They grumble still; and if they lose,
1350 There are no means a man might use
Whereby their grudge could be appeased.
Thus they are every way displeased:
For neither wealth nor indigence
Can train them to obedience
And willingness, in any wise;
And many a time they will despise
Good fortune just as much as bad,
As if no human reason had
Survived the pride which makes them blind.

1360 And there are lovers of this kind

Exactly, who, although they get
All they could wish from love, will yet
Find cause to grumble in some way,
And will not faithfully obey
The laws of loving, as they should;
And if they lack a thing they would
Enjoy, forthwith they feel such pain
That obstinately they complain
Of bad luck – always curse and cry
Because their hearts will not comply,   1370
And bear the bad till good befall.
Therefore, if thou art one of all
Who have behaved in such a way,
My son, in your confession, say;
And tell me fully what thou art.

GOWER:

My father, I acknowledge part
Of what you have described above
Of murmur and complaint in love:
Seeing no prospect of success,
I do cry out with bitterness   1380
Against my luck – as who might say,
Continually. And many a day,
Moreover, having seen or heard
My lady's sullen look or word,
Then I complain upon the spot;
And yet to speak I venture not,
For fear my lady be annoyed,
Though all my heart's ease be destroyed:
Thus full of murmur and of fret,
God knows, I drink-in my own sweat;   1390
And though I give no outward sign,
Rebellious is this heart of mine.
And in this manner I confess
To that which you call stubbornness:

Now tell me your opinion.

CONFESSOR:

Thus do I counsel thee, my son:
However other matters stand,
Always conform to love's command,
As far as in your power lies;
1400   For many a time, in many a wise,
Obedience in love prevails
At hours when manly vigour fails.
A strong example proves it so;
And this – if thou shouldst care to know –
Is chronicled for all to find,
And has just come into my mind.

[*The 'strong example' proves to be the Tale of Florent,
which is basically the same as Chaucer's* Wife of Bath's Tale.
*Gower's version differs, however, in some details: Florent is not
one of King Arthur's knights, but 'nephew to the emperor';
his trouble begins not with a sordid rape but with slaying the
son of an officer who later captures him; Florent sees no
dancers in the forest, before meeting the old hag; Gower –
surprisingly enough – omits the hag's lectures on poverty, age,
and* gentilesse, *but includes an account of how she had been
enchanted; finally, the alternative that she offers Florent is, in
Gower, whether she shall be hideous by day and lovely by night,
or the reverse. The tale, with its climax in Florent's good
faith and humility, here requires little more than illustrative
quotation, as for instance of the passage describing Florent's
future bride (l. 1675 ff.*):

He saw the old hag where she sat,
And a more loathsome thing was that
Than ever met the human eye:
Her nose was flat, her eyebrows high;
Tiny her eyes, and deeply set;
With dripping tears her cheeks were wet,
And wrinkled as an empty skin,

70

And they hung down upon her chin;
Her lips had shrunk, she was so old.
She had no beauties to behold:
Her forehead narrow, her locks hoar
(And she peers out as does a Moor),
Her shoulders curving, her neck short,
Such as no pleasure could support;
Her body thick, by no means small;
And, shortly to describe her all,
Never a limb without a lack.

Florent, however, overcomes his revulsion, and has his reward.
The Confessor sums up:]

CONFESSOR:

Therefore, my son, if thou dost right,   1862
Thou shalt thy lady-love obey,
And follow her in every way.

GOWER:

My holy father, so I will;
Such cogencies of reason fill
The instance that has gone before,
That I shall now and evermore
Hereafter all the better serve
In Love's obedience, and observe   1870
My duties towards him. If beside
All this there still are forms of pride
Which you would have me now confess,
Let me know all their inwardness,
My father, and ask on, I pray.

CONFESSOR:

Hear now, my son, what I shall say:
Another of Pride's company
Remains, and is called Surquidry;*
Whereof thou soon shalt hear, to see
If thou art culpable or free,   1880

* Presumption. See also l. 2021.

71

In form and manner as I tell.
Now, understand the matter well,
For Surquidry we call that sin
Of Pride which holds third place within
His court, and never yet has known
The truth till he was overthrown.
For 'Had I known' will oft replace
All his good fortune and his grace,
Since he does everything by guess,
1890 And could not value safety less.
He thinks no kind of counsel fit
Unless himself arrived at it;
His wisdom – in his own conceit –
Alone puts all men's to defeat;
For pride so permeates his thought,
He sets all other wits at naught,
And finds his own deserts so rare,
He thinks himself beyond compare,
He is so seemly, fair, and wise.
1900 Thus he would bear away the prize
Above all others – not that he
Will once, therefor, say *grand merci*
To God from whom all blessings flow;
Upon himself he squanders, so,
His every thought, as if there were
No God of power anywhere:
But he relies on his own wit
Until he falls into the pit
So deeply that he cannot rise.

1910 And thus it is, not otherwise,
He sets his pride of heart above
The justice that is due to love;
Let it be plainly understood,
He is as able and as good
As any, to love any queen:

72

So, nothing noted or foreseen,
He often swings his axe so high
That the chips fall into his eye.
And often he will think that he
Is well-belovéd as can be   1920
By one who really loves him ill.
Now, my son, tell me what thou will
Of all that I have talked about.

CONFESSOR: *(GOWER:)*

GOWER:

Oh father, do not be in doubt:
For certain, there is no man less
(Of any kind of worthiness)
Sure of his worthiness than I,
To be beloved. I do not try
To make it an excuse for me
That unto all men love is free: 1930
Though, truly, no man may prevent
What is so shy and reticent
That it lurks deep in a man's heart;
Yet I shall not grow lax, and start
To think myself in proper case
To love, save by my lady's grace.
But, sir, if what you really mean
Is that in fancy I have been
Loved where in truth no love was shown,
Then I am guilty there, I own.   1940

CONFESSOR:

My good son, tell me in what way.

GOWER:

Now hearken, then, and I shall say,
Good father, what I mean, and how.
Often it has occurred ere now
That through uncertain hope I let

73

Expectancy be vainly set
To trust in things that came to naught,
Being no more than my own thought.
For as it seems that bells reply,
1950 As if with words, to what men cry,
And answer neither more nor less,
To you, my father, I confess,
Such will has overthrown my wit
That every hope which I admit,
Will many a time seem truth to me,
But come to nothing, finally.
And thus I well may say, who can,
That dreaming beguiles many a man;
So it has me, as well I know:
1960 For if a man puts out to row
And has a riven-bottomed boat,
Assuredly he will not float.
That is what dreams have done for me;
For nearest though I thought to be,
And as my dearest dreams portended,
Then I was farthest when all ended –
And like a fool unbent my bow
In all my fancies' overthrow.
Therefore, my father, as to this,
1970 Because my dreams have done amiss
By reason of Presumption, give
My penance to me while I live.
But if you can in any way
Recount me such a tale as may
So paint the sin that I abhor it
Then I shall be the better for it.

[*The Confessor thereupon tells the Tale of Capaneus, which Gower probably derived from the* Thebais (Books Three to Ten) *of Statius. Capaneus was so presumptuous as to insult the gods, and was therefore slain by a thunderbolt from heaven. A second story follows.*]

CONFESSOR:

And, to speak more of Surquidry,   2021
There used to be* in Hungary
In days of long ago, a King
Honest and wise in everything.
So it befell upon a day –
And it was in the month of May –
This King, as at that time men used,
Had had his chariot produced;
And, this luxuriously arraying,
In it he then rode forth a-maying,   2030
Out of the town in jollity
With lords and great nobility
And many merry folk and young –
Whereof some played and others sung,
And some would walk and others ride,
And some would spur their mounts aside
Or guide their horses in and out.
Meanwhile the monarch cast about
His eyes until at last he could
See, making where his chariot stood,   2040
Two pilgrims, old and sere of hue –
So pale and dry that to the view
Like ancient idols they appeared;
Hoary they were, and white of beard,
As is a bush bestrewn with snow;
And nature had not far to go,
But that they seemed entirely dead.
These two approached the King, and pled
For some small gift in charity;
And he, with great humility,   2050
Leapt from his chariot to the ground
And in his arms the pilgrims wound,
And kissed the two, both foot and hand,
Before the nobles of his land,

* This tale may also be found in the *Gesta Romanorum*.

And from his goods supplied their need,
And, when he had performed this deed,
Mounted his chariot again.
What murmurs then, and what disdain,
And what complaint on every side!
2060 Each noble, full of his own pride,
Said to his neighbour, 'What is this?
Our King does very much amiss,
So to abuse his royalty
In public and so visibly,
And thus to make himself so small
To men of no regard at all.'
Such words as these passed to and fro
Among that company; but no
Man openly, and to the King:
2070 Behind his back they said the thing.
The brother of the King was there;
And great offence, at this affair,
He took at once, and laid the same –
Or even greater – scorn and blame
On his liege lord, as all the rest;
Then to the nobles he professed
That later, when he had the chance,
He would leave out no circumstance
In what he laid before the King.

2080 Now hear the outcome of the thing.
Merry and fair were day and weather;
The people laughed and played together
And told each other ever anew
How freshly all the flowers grew,
How greenly all the leaves had sprung;
And then how love, when one was young,
Began to wake the heart, and how
All birds had found their mates by now:
And in this manner having spent
2090 The whole of May Day, home they went.

No sooner was the King at home
And into his own chamber come,
Than there his brother should appear
To pour the tale into his ear:
How he had brought himself to shame
By cheapening his royal name.
To abase himself in such a style
As, to a wretch so poor and vile,
To condescend thus lowlily
Down from his noble dignity;   2100
He must give up such acts as these,
And must make his apologies
To all the lords about his throne.
The King stood still as any stone,
And lent an ear to all this lore;
And, saying little, thought the more.
Nevertheless, to what he heard,
The King returned this courteous word,
That everything should be amended.
And by the time all this has ended,   2110
The cloth lies ready on the board:
In goes the King, with many a lord,
To sit at supper in the hall;
Then, supper being over, all
Take leave of him, and go their ways.
Now in his mind the King surveys
The means by which he may chastise
That brother who could so despise,
In his officious Surquidry,
A praiseworthy humility,   2120
And therefore offered to his lord
Advice that was to be abhorred.
And so, the better to enlighten him,
The King resolves that he will frighten him.

It happened that, when this King reigned,
His country's statutes had ordained

A brazen trumpet, stern of breath;
Now, this was called the Trump of Death,
And in the royal court there was
2130　A man who had this Trump of brass –
Had it in charge and use – whereby,
When any lord deserved to die,
This dreadful trumpet must be blown
Before his gates, to make it known
He had been judged unfit to live;
And such lords, no one might forgive.
By night, then, did this King send for
The trumpeter, and hard before
The brother's gate he bade him sound.
2140　The trumpeter, in duty bound,
Went forth to do his sovereign's word.
The brother knew, when he had heard
Before his gates that stormy blast,
That all his hope of life was past,
For he had not the law to learn.
For help, he knew not where to turn,
But summoned all his friends, to whom
He told the manner of his doom.
They asked him what the cause might be;
2150　But ignorant of the true cause, he
Knew none. They sorrowed then indeed,
For at that time the law decreed
Such power to the Trumpet-call
That they could not conceive at all
How to resist in any way:
Death was the price that he must pay
Unless, indeed, he could obtain
The mercy of his Sovereign.
On this, each exercised his wit
2160　Until they were resolved on it.

A worthy wife this lord had wed,
And this good lady viewed with dread

Her husband's death; and they had five
Children, moreover, left alive –
Of tender years, as it would chance,
And in their form and countenance
Pleasant and beautiful to see.
So they resolved that he and she
Should take their children, on the morrow,
With all appearances of sorrow   2170
(And, but for shirt and shift, no dress,
To move his heart to tenderness)
And pray for the King's pardoning grace
So that the death need not take place.
And thus they spent a woeful night;
Then, at the earliest glimpse of light,
They took the road, in such array
As thou already heardst me say –
All naked, save for shirts alone.
Wildly they wept and made their moan,   2180
Their tresses hanging round their ears:
With sobbing and with bitter tears,
Humbly enough that lord walked then,
Noblest and proudest, once, of men;
And all the citizens who saw
The sight, were full of grief and awe.
But openly to all men's eyes,
Lamenting thus, and with such cries,
Forth with his children and his wife
He fared, a suppliant for his life.   2190
They reached the Court; and in that place,
When men had seen their sorry case,
And noted it, then not an eye
Among the viewers remained dry,
So piteously did they show.
The King pretends, in all this woe,
That nobody knows less than he;
Nevertheless, at his levee,
Men tell him all that has occurred;

79

2200 And, this strange matter being heard,
At last he goes into the hall.
Down on their knees at once they fall
To see what mercy they may meet;
And he beholds them at his feet,
And asks them what they have to fear,
That they kneel so forlornly here.
Then, 'Ah, lord, mercy!', said his brother,
'As to the cause, I know none other,
Except that last night, very late,
2210 The Trump of Death was at my gate,
In token that I must not live:
We come to pray that you forgive
The fault, and set my death aside.'

'O fool, thou art,' the King replied,
Unto his brother, 'much to blame –
And for thy little faith, the same –
That, only for a trumpet-blast,
Through all the town you go aghast,
Thou and thy lady, in such gear,
2220 With all thy little children here,
For all the populace to view.
As to thy speech, it seems that you
Fear death according to man's law,
Though what men say, they may withdraw,
And all its power cease to be:
No more, now, think it strange of me,
Down from my chariot to alight
When there was brought before my sight
By men of such antiquity
2230 My own sure death, in effigy –
What God's, and Nature's, laws intend,
I am not able to amend.
For well I know that unto these
Two men's, my own estate agrees:
All, being flesh and blood, must die.

And thus, although I may comply
With laws which even kings lie under,
It should not be so great a wonder
As thou art, who without good cause
Goest in such dread of man-made laws –   2240
It is a jest to be afraid
Of things which thou mayst well evade.
Hereafter, then, I counsel thee,
My brother – since thou showest me
That men can cause thee fear so sore –
With all thy being, fear God more.
For all shall die, and all shall pass,
No less the lion than the ass,
No less the beggar than the lord;
All with one aspect and accord   2250
Shall death receive them.' Thus the King,
Most wisely, in his reasoning
Both taught his brother and forgave.
And so, my son, if thou wouldst save
Thy virtue, live not sinfully;
Pray meekly for humility,
That thou be not presumptuous.

GOWER:

My father, I am amorous;
And for this reason I beseech
Some instance from you that may teach   2260
Me how love stands in this affair.

CONFESSOR:

My son, I make thee now aware
That both in loving and in all,
If any surquidry befall,
Then ill indeed it may betide
That man who knows this vice of pride,
Which can make dreamers of the wise
And turn straightforwardness to lies,

Through folly of imagination.
2270 And, for thy further information,
That as I have advised thee thou
Mayst shun this vice, I tell thee now
A tale that comes from days of old,
One that the learnéd Ovid* told.

There was a lord's son, long ago,
Whose ingrained pride had made him so
Fastidious, that in all the wide
World's realm he had not found a bride
Worthy his body or his love:
2280 So high he thought himself above
All other creatures, in his state
And in his beauty, that with hate
He viewed all women – there was none
With him to bear comparison.
Narcissus was this young lord's name:
No strength of love could ever tame
His heart, for it was free and wild;
Yet in the end he was beguiled:
And Cupid brought the thing about.
2290 One day, it happened he fared out
In all his circumstance of pride,
And came into a woodland ride,
Among companions of his sort,
Assembled there to hunt and sport.
And when he comes upon the place
Appointed to begin the chase,
Out from their leashes are let go
The hounds, and horns begin to blow.
So the tall stag at last is found
2300 Setting swift feet upon the ground;
Narcissus, spurs in horse's sides,
Makes every haste he can, and rides

* Gower found this tale also in *Metamorphoses*, Book Three.

Till all are left behind. As he
Rode on, he saw a linden tree
Beside a rock; and there below,
He saw a pleasant well-spring flow.
Now, it was wondrous hot that day,
And such a thirst upon him lay
That he must either die or drink.
So down he got, and by the brink   2310
He tied his horse up to a branch,
And lay down on the ground to stanch
His thirst. Into the water then
He looked, nor turned away again:
He saw his own face mirrored there;
And yet, as though the image were
That of some nymph or faëry maid,
Now was his heart by love assayed,
And folly seized upon his mind;
For he believed (as we shall find)   2320
It was a woman that he saw.
The nearer her he tried to draw,
The nearer she approached him too;
He never knew what he should do:
For when he cried, he saw her cry:
And when he called, then her reply
Would echo the same word again.
And thus began the novel pain,
So foreign to him once: for love
With him a cruel bargain drove,   2330
To set his heart upon a thing
For ever beyond compassing.
He, with continual humble prayer,
Begs her come out and join him there;
Sometimes departs as if he spurns
The nymph; but ever again returns,
And she has never changed her place.
He weeps, he calls, he pleads for grace

From that which in its gift has none.
2340 Until against the rocky stone,
As one whose hope and thought were fled,
He dashed himself till he was dead.
Then came the nymphs of stream and well,
And others who in forests dwell,
And found him lifeless where he lay;
So, out of purest pity, they
Dug him a grave beneath the grass,
And buried him. It came to pass
That soon, from where he lay entombed,
2350 Flowers of wondrous beauty obloomed
In such profusion that men might
Well draw a moral from the sight
And from the deeds that he had done –
As there and then was seen. My son,
These flowers in the winter's cold
Alone are fresh and fair: behold,
As this is nature's contrary,
So was his foolish surquidry.

Thus he that held love in disdain
2360 Was brought unto the greatest pain;
And as he set his price most high,
So was least worthy in love's eye
And made most foolish as to wit;
And people still remember it.
Thou, and all others, well might take
Good heed, then, for Narcissus' sake.

GOWER:

My father, in what touches me,
This is a sin I mean to flee,
For pride produces misery;
2370 But in those things especially
Which Love breeds up to weal or woe,

84

Myself I never prided so.
And yet, would God send grace to me,
That with the eyes with which I see
My lady, I were seen by her,
Then in my love, as I aver,
No sort of pride should find a place.
But I am nowhere near such grace;
And so I speak of here and now:
I would both pray you, and allow,   2380
To ask me further about Pride,
If there be other points, untried,
Whereof I should and must be shriven.

CONFESSOR:

By God, my son, be thou forgiven,
If thou hast ever done amiss
In anything concerned with this.
Yet still there is another style
Of Pride, that must be talking while
Words may be said in his own praise.
Nothing can tame his tongue; it sways   2390
As does the clapper of a bell.
Of this, if thou wouldst have me tell,
Then it is fit that thou be told,
So that thy tongue may be controlled
In all men's presence, and win grace –
Which is denied, in many a place,
To men, unable to sit still,
Who otherwise would have their will.
This vice, then, Boastfulness by name,
Is one of those whom Pride can claim   2400
As friend, so that his worth grows less
The more he runs into excess
By acting his own herald. What
Was good to start with, then is not;
What earned him thanks, now earns him blame;

All his repute, and all his name,
Because of boastfulness and pride,
He causes to be vilified.
I read, too, how this boastful sin,
By nature, is the origin
Of that wind by whose blasts, when blown,
A man's good fame is overthrown,
Whose power and virtue, otherwise,
To the world's profit should arise;
But he destroys it cruelly.
There are, of just this quality,
Some lovers too; therefore, if thou
Art one of them, inform me now:
When thou wast given anything
At love's hand – as a gem, or ring –
Or clad thyself against the cold
In some kind word thou hast been told
Of token, friendly look, or letter,
Whereof thy heart has been the better
Because thy lady greeted thee:
Hast thou, for very pride and glee,
Been boastful of it here and there?

GOWER:

Father, would God you were aware
How sure and free my conscience is!
I never had such things as this,
Whereof my heart might be content;
No, not so much as that she sent
By mouth the message 'Greet him well'.
Hence there is nothing I could tell,
Did I incline to boastfulness;
It stands to reason that, unless
I turn to lying, I shall never
Make any boast of love whatever.
I cannot say what I would do
If I had such occasions to

86

As you have mentioned, many a one;
Yet all my life I have found none
But scorn,* which nearly rang my knell:
Of that I have enough to tell;
No other boast can I invent,
So have no reason to repent.
Ask of my life in something more:
I am not guilty on this score.

CONFESSOR:

Son, I am glad that this is so;
For it is urgent you should know 　　　　2450
That, in pure justice, Love makes war
On this vice – on no other more;
Puts all his heart into debate
With it, and holds it most in hate.

[*And now the Confessor tells the story of Alboin and Rosemunda. Alboin, King of the Langobardi, has defeated and killed the King of the Gepidae, Gurmund. He has taken Gurmund's skull and made a cup of it, and has also captured and married Rosemunda, the dead King's daughter. But Alboin gives a feast, at which Rosemunda is made to drink from her father's skull, and Alboin boasts of her submission. In revenge, Rosemunda cuckolds Alboin and, after his death, flees with her lover – only, at last, to be condemned with him to death by poison. The Confessor again sums up:*]

CONFESSOR:

All this was caused by boastful pride.
Better, then, for a man to hide
His self-esteem; for, should he speak,

* The original has here 'daunger', or danger. There is no single word in modern English equivalent to the complex meaning of 'daunger'. It represents all those influences that hinder the lover's suit – influences of both circumstance and character. Chiefly, however, it represents the lady's own stand-offishness, disdain, timidity, prudence, or capriciousness. It also involves a kind of *mana* emanating from the lady's chastity or virginity.

2650 His friends may well be far to seek.
In arms, no boasting will advance
Him who is eager to enhance
His name, and do some famous deed;
Likewise in love, he who would speed
Must keep his tongue from boast and vaunt.
Whatever man that sin may haunt,
Full often will his purpose fail;
He who in battle would prevail,
Or would see Love's rewards attained,
2660 His wagging tongue must be restrained,
The key that keeps his name secure.
Therefore, my son, be ever sure
That you have given this matter heed.

GOWER:

Dear father, thank you; for indeed
Your school is full of gentle lore.
If there are any matters more,
Concerning pride, I should eschew,
Ask on, and I will follow you
In all you bring before my mind.

CONFESSOR:

2670 My son, there is another kind
Of sin that appertains to pride,
Which, like a falcon tall-enskied,
Soars to the summit of delights
That pleasure in his sin excites,
And pays no man's advice respect
Till down he tumbles and is wrecked.
Vainglory is that vice's name;
Whereof, my son, it is my aim
To speak, and give such details of it
2680 That thou mayst learn thereby, and profit.
This prideful vice that is Vain Glory
Does not remember Purgatory:

The joys of this world are so great,
Heaven seems no more to contemplate;
The pomp of life his bastion:
Yet he shall die, when all is done.
He takes but little thought for this,
For all his lust and pleasure is
In things new-fangled, proud, and vain –
As many as he may obtain.   2690
I swear, if he had means to make
His body new, then he would take
Another shape, and leave the old:
No matter what he may behold
Which to us common folk is strange,
He will his former fashion change
At once, and take new colours on –
Like unto the Chameleon
Which, when it sees a different hue
Straightway must change its own anew –   2700
And often in this foolish way
Stands in ephemeral array.
More sprightly than a bird in May,
And fresh and brilliant every day,
A man of this kind changes so
That others think all gay folk go
Like him – and him as model take.
As well as carols, he can make
Rondeaux, ballades, and virelais:
If, added to all this, he may   2710
Succeed in love, his spirit swells
With over-gladness; he foretells
No end of his, and feels no fear,
And thinks no death is drawing near.
For it is always then high tide;
And love has bred in him such pride,
He thinks his joy will never cease.
Now shrive thee, son, in Our Lord's peace,
And of thine own love tell me plainly

2720 If thou thyself hast gloried vainly.

GOWER:

Father, I neither shall nor may
Excuse myself in every way
Of having been vainglorious;
For love's sake I have sometimes thus
Been better furbished and arrayed;
And many a time I have assayed
Rondeau, ballade, and virelai
For her on whom my passion lay;
And these my carols I would paint
2730 With curious words and phrases quaint,
To set my purposes aloft,
And sing them many a time and oft
In halls and chambers round about,
Where I made merry among the rout;
But never yet gained anything.
Thus vainly did my glory spring
From all the joys I could invent;
For when, to make us gay, I meant
To sing her songs of love, instead
2740 They were not made for her, she said,
And would not let a note be heard,
Nor even listen to a word.
So, as to how I stand, I say
That never yet was I so gay,
Nor made so good a song of love,
That I was lifted up above
And had occasion to be glad.
But fear, though, I have often had,
For sorrow that she says me nay.
2750 Nevertheless, I will not say
I have no joy of any sort;
For that which lays all bare – Report –
Lets me, all day, on all sides, hear
Men speaking of my lady dear:

Of how she bears away the prize;
How she is fair, how she is wise;
How womanly her bearing is.
And when I come to hear all this,
What wonder if my bosom swell?
And also when I have heard tell   2760
Good news about her happiness –
Though I be banished, none the less
I count myself most fortunate.
For when I know her good estate,
For the time being (I will swear)
I cannot feel the hurts of care.
I take my pleasure in this way.
But, father, of your wisdom, say –
For in such things you are well taught –
If in all this I have done aught   2770
To make you think of blaming me.

CONFESSOR:

What thou hast done, I pardon thee,
My son (*said he*), and for thy good,
That it be plainly understood,
About this topic thou shalt hear
A story, whence it shall appear
How this proud vice has been abhorred,
In His high justice, by the Lord –
Who wreaks good vengeance on it, too.
Hear now a tale that shall be true;   2780
And though it be not of Love's kind,
Strong is the warning thou shalt find.

[*What follows is derived from the Book of Daniel iv: it is an
extremely faithful paraphrase of Nebuchadnezzar's second
dream, of Daniel's divination, and of the sequel. Little is
worth presenting here, except the account of Nebuchadnezzar
in the guise of an ox:*

　　Then was he glad of the cold grass,

Who loved hot spices in his day;
All his delights were stolen away:
The wine he had been wont to drink,
He swallowed from the well-spring's brink,
Or from the ditch, or from the slough,
And did not look for better now;
Instead of chambers well-arrayed,
Was glad to have a bush's shade;
Had the hard ground to lie upon,
For other pillows found he none;
Shower and storm beat down on him,
And the winds blew on every limb;
He was tormented day and night
By the high God of Heaven's might,
Until, when seven years were past,
He looked upon himself at last:
Instead of dishes, grass and straws;
Instead of hands, an eagle's claws;
A bestial body met his eye,
No man's. Then he began to sigh
For precious gems and cloth of gold
In which he decked himself of old;
And looking on his hide of hair,
He wept the tears of his despair,
As up to heaven he raised his face . . .

Therefore, says the Confessor:]

CONFESSOR:

3043   Therefore, my son, watch heedfully:
So govern thine humanity
That thou become not bestial;
And, wouldst thou live in virtue, all
Thy care must be for humbleness:
Then wert thou safe from all distress.
Or put the case another way:
3050   To proud men, love has naught to say;

92

For even if a woman please
The man, his pride can take no ease.
No man alive can blame too much
A sin of which the shame is such.

[*After a brief introduction, in similar terms, the Confessor
embarks upon the story of Wise Petronella,* or The Three
Questions. There was once a King of Spain, called Alfonso,
who was greatly proud of his wisdom and intelligence, and was
jealous of intelligent rivals, especially of a certain knight, Don
Pedro. Eventually he challenged this knight, on pain of death
and disinheritance, to answer three set questions within three
weeks. The questions were: 'What has least need of human
help, yet is the most tended of all things? What is of most
value, yet costs a man least? What is of least value, yet costs a
man most?' The knight was puzzled, but was rescued from his
distress by his favourite child, his clever and bewitching
daughter — fourteen years old — Petronella. She humbly
offered to confront the King and answer the questions. And so
she did, as follows: 'That which has least need of human help,
yet is most tended by Man, is Mother Earth; that which is of
most worth to a man, yet of least cost, is humility; that which
is of least worth and of highest cost, is pride.' These answers so
satisfied the King that he advanced her father and married the
girl. Thus were humility and wisdom rewarded. Let us all,
therefore, eschew the sin of Pride. The Lover replies:*]

GOWER:

My father, I shall treasure all
That here you put into my mind;
And if one may, by some such kind
Of humble bearing, satisfy
One's love, hereafter I shall try.   3430
But now I beg your further gift
Of questioning in this my shrift.

* The source of this tale appears to be untraceable.

CONFESSOR:

That, my good son, I mean to do.
Now hear, and pay attention too;
For in this business of Pride,
All that I could I have supplied,
In point of sin; in point of love,
You have been well-informed above.
So there is nothing more to say
3440 Of that; but of another way
Of sinning, Envy, I shall tell:
Whose very nature is from hell,
Thus without reason to undo
Its own and others' fortunes too.
And so hereafter thou shalt learn
All kinds of Envy in their turn.

Book Two: Envy

CONFESSOR:

AFTER the vice of Pride there goes
A second; many grievous woes
To other folk he bears about
Within himself, but not without.
For in his thought is endless fire;
If men have more of their desire
(Or are more virtuous) than he,
Or stand above him in degree:
Thence comes his fever and his flame.
Hot Envy is that vice's name.   10
Therefore I ask thee, son, if thou
Hast ever been one, or art now,
Of those whose hearts have known distress
Because of other men's success:
Remember that I speak of love.

GOWER:

So help my cause Our Lord above,
Yes, father, and a thousand-fold.
When I have happened to behold
A lover gay and of good cheer,
Etna – that burns from year to year –   20
Was not so hot as I grew, for
The burning of that secret sore
My heart and thought had bred in me.
The ship that runs along the sea,
And winds and waters overpower,
Is not more troubled in that hour
Than I am if I chance to see
Another who surpasses me
In luck of love and fortune's gift.

95

30 But, father, I declare in shrift,
All this is one single place;
For he who gains or loses grace
Elsewhere, can never make me grieve.
This also you may well believe:
So utterly my heart befools me
About my lady, she who rules me,
That though I knew I were to die,
Restrained I could not be when I
Saw coming to my lady's side
40 The Court of Cupid in their pride
Of pleasant gaiety and wit –
Though they get never a rush by it
But speaking and to hear her speak,
My sorrow is not far to seek.
But when they whisper in her ear,
Then grows the worst of all my fear;
And oh! if they should whisper long,
Then are my sorrows grown so strong
Because those others are at ease,
50 I cannot speak of my unease.
As to my Love herself, however,
Though ten or twelve should woo her, never
For any lack of trust in her
Should I be grieved; for truly, sir,
In word and deed, the wide world round,
I think no woman could be found
More wary of what she is about –
Nor subtler, as I make no doubt,
At all times to preserve her honour
60 And yet draw gratitude upon her.
Confessed, however, let it be,
That when at any time I see
(Or even if I chance to hear)
That she makes any man good cheer:
Though I may interfere with naught,
I soon disturb the man, in thought.

For though myself be set apart,
Envy works changes in my heart,
So that I feel it full of woe
To see another gladdened so   70
By her; but as to others, all
That to their lovers may befall
(Whether they sorrow or succeed),
To that I pay but little heed.
Now all, my father, has been said
By me on this especial head,
As far as lay within my skill.
Ask on, my father, what you will.

CONFESSOR:

My son, before I so proceed,
I think it well that thou shouldst heed   80
A small example of this kind
Of Envy, to improve thy mind.
Often I have heard fables* say
That though it is not a dog's way
To feed on chaff, he will prevent
An ox from taking nourishment,
Who enters barns in search of it.
Thus, it is plain to wise men's wit,
It goes with Love, in many a place:
For he who is in Love's disgrace   90
And for himself may not prevail,
Will often hope that others fail;
And, given a chance, is full of zeal
To put a spoke into their wheel.
They come in more than tens or twelves,
Those who are powerless for themselves
In love, and enviously spy
How best all others to deny:

* The original has here 'Write in Civile': 'written in the Civil
Law'. Gower must mean that he took this fable from some com-
mentary upon the Institutes of Justinian.

And I have read, and thou shalt hear,
100 A tale that makes my purpose clear.

[*This is the well-known tale of Acis and Galathea, and of
Polyphemus's envy. It may be found, apart from one or two
minor additions by Gower, in Ovid's* Metamorphoses, *Book
Thirteen. The Lover hastily brushes aside his Confessor's
warning summary.*]

GOWER:

211 Father, I find this instance good;
But howsoever matters stood
With Polyphemus long ago,
Love never shall affect me so
That I commit a felony
Through having to love enviously.
Therefore, if other points there be,
As soon as you explain to me
Their nature, then I shall confess
220 And shrive me to your holiness.

CONFESSOR:

Good son, there rests a vice which is
The very opposite of this –
That Envy who can take delight
In looking at the sorry plight
Of other men; who best will fare
When he observes the grief and care
Of other people in their fall,
And so feel high above them all.
Such are the joys that Envy picks
230 From worldly strife and politics;
And very often he will do
Just so in amorous matters too.
If thou, my son, hast therefore had
Pleasure at seeing others sad,
Confess it now.

GOWER:

My father, yes;
That is a thing I must confess.
Those men whose love is strenuous
And, for what makes them covetous,
Are prosecutors year by year
In Courts of Love – when I may hear   240
How they mount up on Fortune's wheel
And think their joy beyond repeal,
Only to be hurled down at last:
Then I feed well because they fast,
And laugh because I see them lour.
And thus, because they have brewed sour,
My drink is sweet; and I am eased
Because I know they are displeased.
But all this that I tell you here
Is only for my lady dear;   250
Where other ladies are concerned
I care not who is overturned
Nor who may stand upon the height.
But be they squire or be they knight
Who dog my lady and would woo,
The more they lose what they pursue,
The more it seems to me I win
And am the happier, here within,
For knowledge of their miseries.
Because, in cases such as these,   260
It always is – men say – relief
To one who is enwrapped in grief,
To find another in like pain,
And join their voices to complain.
It helps me, when I lose my labour,
To see the travails of my neighbour;
And I rejoice at every let.
For though I profit nothing, yet
His sorrow fills my heart with glee;

99

270 When I reflect that it is he
Who views my lady with affection
But gains no ground in that direction,
I think it merry as a game.
If such an envy be to blame
(And I confess to feeling it)
You who are wise, and quick of wit,
Must tell me your opinion.

CONFESSOR:

There is no sense or worth, my son,
In Envy; nor can ever be
280 In any species known to me.
For, such is Envy's nature, when
He can do harm to other men,
To this end he will set aback
His own desire, to others' lack,
And spoil their good by losing his.
So as to show you how it is,
There is a story which I deem
Worth telling, on this very theme,
For it will fully illustrate
290 The sin in all its envious hate.

Some authors* I have read record
That one day Zeus, Olympus' Lord,
Determined that mankind's petitions
About their sorrowful conditions
Must be investigated – must
Be satisfied, if they were just.
And for this reason, down he sent
An angel; and the angel went
Round and about upon his way
300 Collecting truth. Until one day
This angel who must make report,

* This tale may be found in the fables of Avian. 'Some authors'
is my own (deliberate) inaccuracy.

And was disguised in human sort,
Had overtaken, so they say,
Two travellers along the way,
By whom he fancied he might be
Informed; and so himself made three.
With cunning words this angel then
Asked many questions of the men;
Till now with harsh words, now with soft,
He set the pair to wrangling oft –   310
And each had plenty to be said.
Thus, by a trick, the angel led
These men, with skilful questioning,
Until he had learnt everything
About the natures of the two;
And in the end the angel knew
That one of them was covetous,
And his companion envious.
The angel, learning this, pretended
To take his leave. Hear how things ended: 320
He said he must go, verily,
But, since it was a deity
That sent him thither, and because
Of all the kindness that there was
In the companionship which they
Afforded him along the way,
He would give joy to them as well.
He said that one of them must tell
What he most eagerly desired;
And he should have what he required;   330
But furthermore, whatever he
Might ask, the other man should be
Most surely given twice as much.
And thus he put them to the touch.

Sir Covetous was wondrous glad,
And to Sir Envious he bade
That *his* desire be first disclosed;

And this he said for he supposed
That wealth would be his friend's demand:
340　How comfortably then would stand
His own case, who would then outright
Take double. In this way, by sleight,
And only in the hope to win,
He bade Sir Envious begin.
Now, Envious, though he was late
To see that he at any rate
Must ask in the first instance, thought
That any fame or wealth he sought
Would cheer his friend in double measure –
350　Which was by no means to his pleasure.
So then he showed in his true light,
This Envious: for in this plight,
There was but one request he made
The angel, and for this he prayed:
That he be blinded in one eye,
So that his friend should nought descry.

And this word was no sooner said
Than one eye perished in his head;
And as for his companion,
360　That instant he was left with none.
Sir Envious was well contented,
And laughed while Covetous lamented;
He paid one eye, and nothing loth,
For his companion to lose both.
And much the same as happened then,
We now hear told of many men:
The world runs more and more awry,
Yet no one knows the reason why;
For it is nature's contrary
370　To compass one's own injury;
Nor can my own good be achieved
In that I see my brother grieved.
What sayest thou to this folly, son?

GOWER:

My father, every lie to shun,
This heart of mine was never set
Upon that kind of sin, as yet,
Except as I have said before.
Nevertheless, if there is more
That in my shrift I ought to say
Concerning Envy, ask, I pray.   380

CONFESSOR:

And that shall certainly be done;
Listen and pay good heed, my son.
I know not one, of all the brood
Of Envy, with a grain of good;
Nevertheless, such as they be,
Here is another: this is he
Whom everybody calls Detraction –
He who, to ratify his action,
Enlists the aid of calumny;
Whose tongue nor Cross nor Pile* can fee   390
So that it utters in men's hearing
One plain good sentence without sneering,
And this behind a fellow's back.
Though he may praise, he finds some lack,
And always leaves it to the last,
So all the good is overcast.
And though there be no reason, that
Is not a hindrance to his chat,
As one who plays the herald's part
For those with falsehood in their heart.   400
For as the nettle thrives and grows
Until it blights the fresh red rose
Into a pale and faded yellow,
Right so this false and envious fellow –
No matter where he comes or dwells –

* The 'heads' and 'tails' of a coin.

With all the falsehoods that he tells,
Turns all his praises into blame,
And honour into open shame.
Such are the lies he will invent,
410   No man so good but will be pent
Between his teeth, and be backbitten,
And see a false indictment written.
He is the shelly beetle's kind,
Among whose habits this I find:
That, in the merry month of May,
About the hottest of the day,
He spreads his wings and up he flies
And all around beneath him spies
The fair and pleasant flowers grow.
420   He takes no pleasure in them, though;
But where he sees that any beast
Has left some filth, he makes his feast;
And thereupon he will alight,
For he enjoys no other sight.
Just so, this babbler, envious
To see a neighbour virtuous
And both in worth and fortune fat,
Will never say a word of that;
But if, however slight it be,
430   There is some scandal he can see,
Then open-mouthed he runs about
Behind a man, and bawls it out;
But every virtue of a man,
That he keeps secret if he can;
Only of vices will he tell –
Like one who went to school in hell,
Envy's own foster-brother, bred
With him in house and board and bed,
Who has for office and for role
440   To plant a sin on every soul.
And though his mouth be fair to view,
Yet all his words come out askew

And are the worst that he can say.
It is not otherwise today
Within the Court of Love, where we
Hear it lamented frequently
That many an envious tale is bruited
That can in no way be confuted
And very often is believed;
And many a worthy love is grieved   450
By false and envious Detraction.

If thou hast set such tales in action,
My son, in Love's Court, now confess.

GOWER:

Assuredly, my father, yes.
Not, I must tell you, openly,
But now and then in privacy,
When I have met my dearest love
And thought how high she is above
My little worth; or when I see
A spry and lusty company,   460
A young and fashionable rout,
All day pursuing her about,
Each of them waiting for his chance
With tales of lying circumstance
To lead astray an innocent
Who will not be of their intent.
Though, since men say 'Unknown, unkissed',
She keeps her thumb within her fist,
So tightly tucked in her own hand
That no man gains an inch of land;   470
And she believes not all they tell,
And guards her self and honour well,
And fears 'If I had only known':
Still, even so, my heart has grown
High. For they love not two or three
Alone, these common lovers: see

Them court in almost every part!
These I have envied in my heart,
And always I must fear their guile
480 In case with cunning and with wile
They may enchant her innocence.
Thus, all I dare in her defence,
I haunt my love with slanders, such
As will not let her trust too much.
What comes into my mouth, I say –
And would say worse, knew I the way.
For when I meet her and may speak,
Since there is much I hope or seek
From such deceit, all is rehearsed
490 To her, especially the worst.
I am so sure that learn she must
How perilous they are to trust,
And what they truly wished and meant
Who were of double-faced intent,
That for all men of evil will
My evil tongue is lusty still.
And what is more, the truth to tell,
For certain if it so befell
That he, of all men born, most true –
500 The one-in-twenty-thousand who
Was trustworthy beyond all doubt –
Were loved by her, and I found out:
Still, rather than that he were sped,
Before my lady I would spread
Such tales about him, if I might,
As should undo his love outright;
And I would do my utmost, too.
For though I told what was not true,
And feigned unthought-of things – be sure,
510 Not for the world could I endure
To see another's full possession
Of fields where I make no impression;
For whether good or bad he be,

She never should be his, for me.
And therefore oft I spy around
And utter words of envious sound,
And try to bring them into blame;
But this is only for those same
To whom my lady seems to draw:
Ever on them I gnash and gnaw,   520
And do them all the harm I may.
But this I do sincerely say:
I speak so to my Love alone,
And not to almost everyone,
Because it is my chiefest care
All speech and gossip to forbear
That may concern my lady's name –
Which, both in earnest and in game,
I shall preserve until my death;
For I would rather lack all breath   530
Than hurt her honour by a word.

And now, my father, you have heard
Whatever touches Love in all
The kinds of speech I have let fall,
And do confess to be detraction:
Instruct me in my further action.
I am quite ready to abide
My punishment, and set aside
Such things as you will not allow:
He who is bound must ever bow;   540
To your commands I so shall do,
For this I dare to promise you,
That I have not concealed a word,
But told you all as it occurred;
My conscience otherwise is free
From every kind of calumny;
Nor do I, in my conscience, find
Envy of any other kind
By which Love's countenance were darkened.

550 Now I have spoken, you have hearkened,
Father, what would you have me do?

CONFESSOR:

Such deeds, my son, thou must eschew,
And let thy tongue be ever still;
So mayst thou better have thy will:
As thou thyself hast said of her,
It is thy lady's character
To be in all things wise and wary;
No slanders then are necessary,
Nor any such misinformation.
560 For when she sees the situation,
And knows how envious thou art,
Thou shalt be farther from her heart
Than else thou mightst be – who can tell?
No man draws water from the well
Wherein he knows a poison lies;
And many a time, when one man tries
To injure others, he will find
That he has been left far behind,
His hopes of victory undone.
570 Therefore thyself beware, good son,
And leave thy wicked speech and thought –
For which revenge was often wrought
On many a man before today:
For he who has touched birdlime may
In no wise keep his fingers clean;
Filth upon filth shall there be seen
That otherwise would not adhere;
This, every wise man ought to fear.
For he who would another blame
580 Shall oft encompass his own shame,
Whereas he might be tranquil still.
So, therefore, if it be thy will
Thy reformation to advance,
A tale of great significance

> For thy sake I propose to tell,
> And it will edify thee well.

[This is the story of Constance, used by Chaucer as the Man of
Law's Tale. *Both poets used the same direct source, Nicholas
Trivet's* Anglo-Norman Chronicle, *and Chaucer himself seems
to have read Gower's version – which is, incidentally, much the
more pedestrian. It is followed immediately by the tale of
Demetrius and Perseus, the sons of Philip of Macedon. The
heir-apparent, Demetrius,* was held to be the better knight; his
brother was therefore bitterly envious, and went to their father
accusing Demetrius of treason. Demetrius was executed, and
Perseus became the heir. He grew so proud that he rebelled
against his father, who soon realized*

> *How Perseus, with his slandering*
> *Tongue, had caused envious bells to ring*
> *Death to Demetrius his brother.*

*Philip was deposed; but Perseus's own downfall was at hand,
one omen being the death of a pet dog of the same name.
At this time, Perseus was at war with the Romans under
Paulus Emilius; and one day he marched forth to do battle.]*

CONFESSOR:

> It fell upon the winter-tide
> That Perseus and his host must ride
> Across the Danube, that great flood.
> All frozen hard the river stood,   1830
> An easy crossing, to his mind.
> But Fortune's wheel was ever blind;
> Its turning takes us unaware:
> That ice the horsemen thought would bear,
> Was shattered; the majority
> Were drowned, of all that cavalry,
> For the rear-guard was swept away
> And none came to dry land that day.
> To Paulus, that good knight of Rome,

* No single source for this tale can be adduced.

1840　Spies bring this information home;
　　　He makes all haste to march away,
　　　So that upon the second day
　　　His soldiers meet, in open plain,
　　　Such of King Perseus' as remain,
　　　With all their banners wide-displayed.
　　　At once his army was arrayed
　　　In battle-order at his back,
　　　And on he marched to the attack,
　　　And slew or captured all he found –
1850　Whence Macedonia, made renowned
　　　For years, by Alexander, lay
　　　Devoured and ruined in a day.
　　　On Perseus only there must fall
　　　The blame, for this misfortune: all
　　　The people of the land exile
　　　His heir; he, in despair the while,
　　　Disguised in rags, is forced to flee
　　　To Rome; and there, penurious, he
　　　Must learn (a craft most common in
1860　Those days) to work in brass and tin,
　　　So as to earn his daily bread.
　　　Such was the son's fate, it is said;
　　　And, of his father, people say
　　　That, a close prisoner, he lay
　　　In jail at Alba, where he died
　　　Because his victuals were denied.
　　　The dog was meant to prophesy
　　　That like a dog should Perseus die,
　　　Who had been dog-like in his action
1870　When he, with envious detraction,
　　　Barked at his brother from behind.

　　　Such are the profits folk may find
　　　When they would hinder other men.
　　　With all your heart and power, then,
　　　Eschew, my son, eschew that vice.

GOWER:

Else were my wits of little price ...

*[The Confessor now turns to another species of Envy – False
Semblance, or Dissimulation, another of the rocks on which
love may be wrecked. Gower denies having practised serious
dissimulation. But, he says, he has now and then*

> *stood in the row*
> *Of those with use for sandalwood*

*– i.e. of those who put a false colour upon things – to discover if
another man is involved with his, Gower's, lady. These are
all he is concerned with; and if by such means he hears any
other secret, he forgets it forthwith. Nevertheless, he doubts if
there is any man who, having seen his lady, has failed to love
her. He himself tells her everything, for with her he can practise
no dissimulation. Nevertheless, he is reproved by his Confessor,
who now proceeds to tell the story of Hercules and Deïanira.]*

CONFESSOR:

False Semblance that has been believed,
Full many a worthy soul has grieved;
Long before *our* birth was it so.
My son, for this cause thou shalt know
A tale told of Dissimulation
Which poisons many a good relation,   2160
And hangs its sail with many a gaud
Of evil counsel and of fraud.
Deïanira* bought it dear,
And Hercules, though both were clear
Of guilt. Now hear the tale I tell
Of how their miseries befell.
She, only, knew how to possess
Hercules' heart with loveliness,
This fair Deïanira; and,

* The story is chiefly from Ovid's *Metamorphoses*, Book Nine.

III

2170 Upon a day, they chanced to stand
Beside a river. Then a need
Was felt by Hercules to lead
His love across with him, although
He had no boat, and did not know
The ford: so he was in distress
For that sweet lady's tenderness.
A certain giant* lived near by,
Nessus by name, who cast his eye
Upon the hero and his bride:
2180 Envy of Hercules supplied
Him then with thoughts of treachery –
Deep in his heart of secrecy
Strong envy holds dominion;
The deed he thinks of, shall be done.
But it is dangerous, he sees,
Against the doughty Hercules,
Openly challenging, to fight.
So, with false semblance, and with sleight,
With friendship feigned, to where they stood
2190 He came, and used what art he could
To seem as charming as can be.
He was at their command, said he,
At any time to serve them well
In any way. And, it befell,
They trusted to him and his lies,
And asked him if he could advise
A way – for some way must be found –
To cross the river safe and sound,
And soon, and never be apart.
2200 While Nessus heard the secret heart
Of their desire, and what it meant,
Then with ambiguous intent
He turned a pleasant face to them;
And he devised a stratagem

* Thus Gower; but Nessus was, of course, a centaur – and is so called by me henceforward.

When he had heard how they would go.
Awhile he feigned a pleasant show
Of services and courtesies;
But very different thoughts were his.

This Nessus, though he spoke in sleight,
Laid arguments before their sight   2210
Which on the surface promised well
And yet within were false and fell.
He warned them to beware, and keep
Eyes open, for the stream was deep
And the ford hard for them to find;
But he, if they were so inclined,
As to accept his help (he said),
Would lend himself to see them sped
In their dilemma: he would make
The passage of the flood, and take   2220
The Lady, setting her once more
Safe down upon the farther shore;
And Hercules, moreover, may
Follow his footsteps all the way.
To this plan everyone agrees;
And well content is Hercules,
Not knowing what is to befall.
The centaur is best pleased of all,
And takes the Lady up aloft
And makes his giant shoulder soft   2230
And, never grumbling at the load,
Wades out into the water-flood.
He bore her over, safe and sound;
But when he stood upon dry ground,
While Hercules was far behind,
He cast his promise from his mind;
For 'Yea' or 'Nay' he took no thought,
But with Deïanira wrought
Like one whose wish was to dissever
The Lady and her Love for ever.   2240

When Hercules became aware
Of the assault, he then and there
Forged on as fast as he could go.
It happened he had brought a bow;
And this, in awful haste, he bent
So as to speed his bolt – and sent
One with old poison on its head.
Timely and true the arrow sped,
And pierced the centaur through and through,
2250   Halting the false deed he would do.

Hear now a deeper villainy:
When Nessus knew that he must die,
He bade the Lady take his shirt –
Which, with the heart's blood of his hurt
Was stained and streaming everywhere –
And keep it by her, with all care
And secrecy, to this intent:
That, if her lord's affections went
A-straying to some newer love,
2260   Then, if she could so much as move
Her lord to wear the shirt, she should
Behold its power, for he would
Look on all other love as vain,
And bring his heart back home again.
The Lady's joy was now entire;
And yet her heart seemed all on fire
Till in her box, and under key,
The shirt was hidden secretly.

The days go by, the years depart,
2270   Colder and colder grows the heart
In one whose loving is untrue.
Hercules falls in love anew,
And sets his heart on Iolë,
As is reported commonly.
This Iolë (the tale runs thus)

Was daughter of King Eurytus,
And so besotted Hercules
With love and loving niceties
And all her maiden comeliness,
That he began to wear her dress,   2280
And she his tunic just as often.
Thus manly powers abate and soften,
And female tenderness prevails;
And no man's remedy but fails.
Surely no dearth of weeping stirred
Deïanira, when she heard;
She knew of nothing else to do:
Straight to her secret box she flew,
Tear-blinded from her bitter hurt,
And out she took that fatal shirt.   2290
She had no thought of doing harm
When she exerted all her charm
Till Hercules pulled on and wore
The shirt; thus Nessus, long before,
Had bidden her, as you have heard;
But, doing so, the Lady erred;
Destiny will not be denied:
So, by False Semblance mystified,
When she was nearest to her goal
(As *she* thought) she let slip the whole.   2300
No sooner is the shirt drawn on
Than it clings fast, and to the bone
Burns Hercules – for it retains
The poisoned blood from Nessus' veins.
Out to the mountain forest ran
Hercules then, like a wild man;
And learnéd Ovid tells that he
Tore down full many a massive tree
In the great fury of his might;
And, that huge pyre being set alight,   2310
He leapt therein – and in a flash
So burnt his flesh and bone to ash.

[The Confessor now turns to the vice of Supplantation. Gower admits that he has often longed to supplant his rivals: but he has never acted upon his wish, nor would he dream of doing so in a dishonest way. After running briefly through three familiar tales* (Agamemnon's theft of Briseis from Achilles, Diomed's seduction of Cressida from Troilus, and the story of Amphitryon's impersonation of Geta), the Confessor turns to one less familiar – that of the Sultán of Persia's daughter.]

CONFESSOR:

2501 Of cities that stand high in fame,
The chief is noble Rome by name;
And, our historian says, before
Christ was its Lord, an emperor
Held there such calm dominion
That wars and conflicts there were none:
For, everywhere that Rome had sway,
No subject dared to disobey;
All was tranquillity and rest.
2510 Some thought all this was for the best;
And others, nothing of the kind –
But these were they whose hearts inclined
To derring-do and chivalry.
That flower of all virility,
The good son of the Emperor,
Most burned to be a warrior;
For he was bold, and covetous
Of worldly fame, and chivalrous:
He went about, then, to implore
2520 His father, 'Let me ride to war
Beyond strange frontiers far away.'
His father told him he must stay,
And would by no means let him roam.
The son, who could not rest at home,

---

* The tales here briefly referred to are easily accessible, with the exception of the last, which has no assignable source.

Sought out a trusted knight of his
And told him all his business
(No word, though, was his father told).
He said that if his luck should hold,
He would be going, by and by,
Upon a journey, and would try   2530
To cross, obscurely, the Great Sea* –
There, for a certain time, to be
In travails and pursuits of war.
The knight, upon his honour, swore
To keep the counsel of his lord,
And vowed he was of one accord.
Now, both of them were young; and hence,
As outcome of their conference,
They both agreed to flee the court.
And so, to make the story short. . . .   2540

[*Let us take him at his word. The prince and his knight
arrive in Cairo to find that the Sultán of Persia is at war with
the Caliph of Egypt. The prince enlists in the Sultán's army,
and speedily wins military renown, spurred on by his love for the
Sultán's beautiful daughter and heir. On the eve of a pitched
battle against the Egyptians, the Sultán removes his daughter's
ring and makes her swear that, if she is left fatherless, she
will marry the man who brings the ring back to her.*]

CONFESSOR:

And now the men of might assemble,   2621
While those with timid hearts must tremble;
Now one man slays, another dies;
And who deserves the richest prize
But Rome's young prince? For where he rides
With deadly sword, no man abides,
And in his presence all must yield;
Before him, Egypt flees the field;
Persia pursues the hunted foe;

* Of course, the Mediterranean.

117

2630   Till, by what chance I do not know,
Behold – an archer's random shot
Smote the Sultán; and on the spot
At once he fell, and there he lay.
No more pursuit was done that day;
They carried him into his tent.
He saw full well how matters went,
And that his days were surely done;
So, to this Knight of Rome (since none
Deserved more trust) his daughter's ring
2640   He gave, and told him everything –
In secrecy all this was spoken –
About her oath and this its token;
And said that she must be his wife.
Thus the Sultán took leave of life:
Soon the heart beat in him no more.
Thereon, as custom was, they bore –
With highest circumstance and care –
His body back to Cairo, where
They laid it in a lordly grave.
2650   The nobles who took heed to save
The Kingdom (which was desolate),
The better to rebuild the state,
Summoned an early parliament.
Hear now what came of their intent.
This youthful knight, this worthy lord
Of Rome, the Council being toward,
Confided in his Bachelor*
And let him see the ring he bore –
With which, as the Sultán had said,
2660   The Persian princess should be wed;
Thus she had vowed to the Sultán
When he received it: by what man
Soever it should be restored,
Him she would take, to be her lord.
'So much is sure,' he said, 'but we

* i.e. his squire, the 'knight' of p.2525

118

Alone know where the ring may be.'
Now this was on the night before
The Assembly. Though our Bachelor
(Who heard the tale with interest,
And had more thoughts than he expressed)   2670
Pretended to be glad, and showed
A mask of smiles, another mode
Of countenance within he wore.
The wise philosophers of yore,
Who studied their own world, have written
That men may soonest be cross-bitten*
By those who most enjoy their trust;
And we may prove the proverb just,
By what befalls this lord of Rome.
By night, the Bachelor has come   2680
To where his youthful master slept,
Filched from the purse where it was kept
The ring with which his lord should wed,
And left another in its stead.
Next morning the Princess was brought
Before the Assembly, where they sought
(When they had sworn their fealty)
To know her mind towards marriage. She,
Remembering her father's will,
And thinking only to fulfil   2690
Her oath, must openly declare
To all, the truth of the affair.
When she had spoken, who was glad
If not our knightly Roman lad?
And so he pulled his purse out on
The instant; but the ring was gone:
It was his Bachelor he saw
Produce it and demand the law.

[*There is no gainsaying the will of the Sultán, and the token of
it. The Bachelor is married and crowned, and the Roman*

* Cheated, gulled.

119

prince falls sick with chagrin. On his deathbed, however, he discloses the truth, both to the assembled lords and (by letter) to his father. A Roman task-force arrests the usurper, who is condemned to death. . . . Another case of Supplantation follows— that of Popes Boniface* and Celestine. According to Gower's version, Boniface, as Cardinal, was envious of Celestine's election. By a species of subliminal persuasion, he induces Celestine to abdicate in favour of himself. But Boniface, after a stormy papacy, is arrested and dies in prison. This is what comes of Envy, because

> *She is the courtiers' common whore,*
> *Keeps open tavern at whose door*
> *They swill a draught that sets on fire*
> *Their hearts, and giddies their desire*
> *To outdo others everywhere,*
> *Be it by foul means or by fair. . . .*

And, with a change of gender:
> *He has no reason to despair*
> *Of being Hell's apparent heir,*
> *The Devil's very next-of-kin,*
> *And farthest from the hope that in*
> *The Heavenly Kingdom he may dwell.*

Therefore:]

CONFESSOR:

3153   To be a lover out of danger,
Let Envy be to thee a stranger.

GOWER:

My holy father, reason is
That I eschew a vice like this;
And yet, if I were stronger still
In spirit, it would not be ill.
If you would tell, I should be glad:
3160   Is no preventive to be had,

---

* It is difficult to say precisely where Gower obtained some of the – occasionally legendary – details of this story.

To keep the vice away from me?

CONFESSOR:

Give heed, my son, and thou shalt see:
As every sickness has its cure,
So virtues make the vices pure.
And reason shows that he who would
Eschew the vices, plainly should
Pursue the virtues; thus he may
See all his vices purged away,
For vice may not with virtue dwell.
We all have seen spring waters quell   3170
The fierce malignancy of flame:
Thus, under virtue, vice grows tame.
Now, Envy's foe is Charity,
The mother of kind Pity – she
Who makes the heart of man so tender
That, where she rules, it may engender
No cruel thought of any kind;
For she so mitigates his mind
That even for his own relief
He will not cause his neighbour grief. ...   3180
This only needst thou understand: 3501
Keep Charity within thy hand,
And thou shalt not be poor in grace.
And, therefore, if thou wouldst embrace
A very sovereign remedy
For envy, dwell with charity
And lock that virtue in thy breast.

GOWER:

My father, I shall do my best.

[The gap indicated above (lines 3181–500) contains an example
of charity in action – the story of the Emperor Constantine and
his leprosy.* Constantine was told that his only cure was to
    * Much of this story is in the Legenda Aurea.

bathe in the blood of infants; but he resolved to bear the disease rather than cause widespread grief. He was told in a vision, that his mercy should have its reward; and so it came about: upon his receiving baptism, the leprosy departed from him. From l. 3508 to the end of Book Two (l. 3530) we have Gower's resolution to eschew Envy, and the Confessor's introduction to Book Three.]

Book Three: Wrath

CONFESSOR:

IF thou wouldst know all sins, my son,
Most alien to the law is one
Well known on earth to human-kind
Since ever men had swords to grind;
And, in the power of this Vice,
Good friends have often, in a trice,
Been maddened by the merest chance.
And yet the Vice does not enhance
Men's pleasure: where it most achieves,
There also most mankind it grieves –   10
And, lacking thought and sympathy,
Is Patience' natural enemy.
One of the seven that many a day
Have led the unsteady world astray,
This Vice's name is Cruel Ire:
His heart is evermore on fire
For harm that he may speak or do.
His servants are all wrathful too.

GOWER:

Good father, say what thing is this
That is called Ire?

CONFESSOR:

       My son, it is   20
In English, Anger: he whose tongue
Has evermore so hotly stung
That all a listener's patience dies,
And flames of violence arise.
Anger has always with him five
Servants to help him rage and strive.

The first is Melancholy;* he
Will find himself in company
And yet a hundred times an hour
30   Will like an angry wild beast lour
While no one knows the reason. Now
Confess to me, my son, if thou
Hast been thus melancholy.

GOWER:
                Aye,
Good father; if I must not lie,
Then, by St Julian I fear
Of this I am not wholly clear.
It is love's fault, as well I know;
Love makes my heart a steady glow,
A burning as of coal, for wrath
40   That love provides no easy path.
Thus, many times a day, for naught
But that which rises from my thought,
I rage against myself; indeed,
However other men may speed
In games of love, I am not glad.
Rather, my anger makes me sad:
It may be sport to others; me
It turns to purest misery.
So dourly am I self-oppressed
50   By thoughts that spring from my own breast,
That in my waking dreams I meet
In private with my lady sweet,
And beg that she will speak me fair;
But since she will not lightly swear,
She says me nay without an oath.
And then I grow so inly wroth

* It is interesting to note that 'melancholy', to Gower, means violent anger and sullenness, as well as mere sadness. This was the current fourteenth-century meaning, and there is an instance of its survival in Shakespeare (*King John*, III, iii, 42).

That I look fearful, and betray
All my displeasure and dismay.
A thousand times a day I hear
That 'No' resounding in my ear,   60
That 'No' I dreamed I heard her speak;
And then my wits are far to seek –
Especially when I begin
To count, and reckon up within,
How many of my years have flown
In faithful love of her alone,
With never another worth my heeding;
And yet no nearer to succeeding,
For all the time I spend on her;
My fortune and my comforter   70
Seems farther off the more I try;
My happiness hangs all awry,
My thoughts are muddied with my care;
And I – a man might say – despair
When in the end I fall to musing
On her implacable refusing:
For then in anger am I clad,
Nor for the world could I be glad.
And all the while I feel my fit,
My joy stands upside down for it;   80
And still the farther off from her
Dear sight I am, the readier
I am in growing choleric:
Then for the dropping of a stick,
Or for a twisting straw, I rave
As does the angry ocean wave –
And grow so melancholy then
That all among my serving-men,
And all about my house, I spread
A very potent fear and dread   90
That I may shortly lose my mind
From anger of so fierce a kind;
So every one, both small and great,

Is troubled till my fits abate.

But, father, if it so betide
That I may ever stand beside
My dearest love in any place,
And then if heaven gives her grace
To spare me a kind word, then not
For all the gold in Camelot*
Could I keep anger in my heart:
How soon my angry moods depart!
So happy in her company
Am I, that every injury
Is pardoned her and set at naught
Against the raptures of my thought.
Nevertheless, if truth be told,
If it should chance that I behold
The contrary – if I should see
Her cast an unkind look at me,
Or if she will not look at all –
If I observe this, then I fall
Straightway into my former state,
And grow so deathly desolate
That all is evil as before.
And thus I pick at my own sore –
And thus have done, on many a day –
And out I go, as go I may,
And many times I bite my lip;
Thus for myself I make the whip
With which, through many a cold and heat,
My own unhappy heart I beat;
And then I have no power to soften
My wits: I rage, God knows how often.
This is all melancholy, grown
From amorous fancies of my own
And love that will not bow the knee;
And thus I bear about with me

100

110

120

---

* The original reads 'Rome', but the substitution was irresistible
– and not merely for the sake of rhyme.

My angry muzzle half the year.
But, father, who are sitting here   130
Love's vicar, from you I beseech
Some moral story that may teach
My anger to endure control.

CONFESSOR:

Son, for the comfort of thy soul,
I shall fulfil thy prayer; and so
That thou shalt all the better know
The mischief which this Vice may cause
For want of pardon or of pause –
Though people afterwards regret
Their folly and, grown sober, let   140
Themselves consider what was done.
Whereof, here is a tale, my son.

There was a King called Aeolus,
Whose fortune had befallen thus:
He had two children fair to see –
The daughter known as Canace,
The son Macarius* by name.
Sister and brother shared the same
Apartment, night as well as day,
When they were young, and there would play 150
Together as all children do.
And this continued while they grew
To that fresh spring of lustiness
When Nature first begins to oppress
The heart with love, and makes it yield
Till Reason's laws are all repealed
And hers have sole authority.
For under Cupid's curacy,

* Gower regularly uses the form 'Machaire', but gives 'Macar-
ius' in the marginal gloss. I have used this in preference to the
more correct 'Macareus'. It may be noted, incidentally, that
Gower uses 'Canace' trisyllabically, but so as to rhyme with his
own disyllabic 'place'.

Since he is sightless, all mankind
160   Must imitate him, and be blind.

Brother and sister, as I say,
Dwelt so together, night and day,
That Nature grew beyond control:
That he, with all his heart and soul,
Beheld her as through lover's eyes.
The end could not be otherwise
Than that, in private meeting thus,
Canace and Macarius
First learned of Cupid how to kiss;
170   Then she who Queen and Mistress is
Of all, and teaches them to live
Without such laws as prelates* give
(For what have they to do with her?
She is her own free arbiter):
Nature, I mean, took them to school
And brought them so beneath her rule –
By both, moreover, freely granted –
That they were, so to speak, enchanted.
And, as blind men by blind are led,
180   And till they fall they fear no dread,
So these two had no inward sight;
But like the bird which will alight
Because, although a snare be set,
He sees the lure and not the net,
They in their youth were unaware
Of danger while the day looked fair;
And so they fell into that state
Where sense and foresight abdicate:
So long this pair cohabited,
190   She grew with child, and shook for dread;
Stayed close within her chamber, lest
Her swelling secret might be guessed

* This refers to 'positive law' – see note on Prologue, l. 247.
Gower's view is that there is nothing in Divine and Natural Laws
against incestuous marriage; but that the *priests* have forbidden it.

And reach the King her father's ear.
And this, too, was her brother's fear:
He feigned a reason, far to ride
Away: he could no more abide
The risk that people might discover
Him to have been his sister's lover:
For she would not as yet declare
Whose child it was that she must bear.   200
The brother went, the sister stayed
And, though not yet in childbed laid,
She had not very long to wait.

Now hearken to her cruel fate.
The matter could not be concealed;
And, being known, it was revealed
At last to Aeolus the King.
And when he had learnt everything,
At once he raged, in such a fit
Of Melancholy as if it   210
Were madness – knowing not, forsooth,
How masterful is love in youth.
As one who held himself apart
From love, he would not move his heart
To mercy and to tenderness
Towards love; but, stern and pitiless,
Mad waves of anger in his mind,
He sought his daughter's room – to find
The infant that she lately bore:
For which (with mighty oaths) he swore   220
That Canace should dearly pay.
Then she began to beg and pray
For pity; knelt on her bare knees,
And sued to him in words like these:
'Have mercy, father! Am I not
Your blood, your child, whom you begot?
The sin whence all these floods have sprung
Came only of my being young

And ignorant of harm or woe.
230 But since my fate befalls me so –
Father, forgive and pity me!'

Her speech forsook her; down fell she,
Swooning for sorrow; and before
His feet she lay, and could no more.
But no soft pity could assuage
His horrible and cruel rage:
Out of the room forthwith he went,
On wrathful vengeance all intent;
And in his heart this thought took shape,
240 That she must die without escape;
For patience cannot hold them when
Such Melancholy captures men
Who suffer anger unconfined.
In this wild anguish, this mad mind,
His very reasoning untamed,
A knight he called to him, and named,
And gave into his hand a sword,
All naked, and therewith this word:
Bearing the sword before him, he
250 Was to repair to Canace.
This message was to be conveyed:
That she must take the sharpened blade
And, if she used her mother-wit,
She would know what to do with it.
Off to his task the knight must go,
To that young woman in her woe;
To Canace the sword he took.
At sight of it, her body shook –
For well she saw what it portended,
260 And well enough she apprehended
The hint it gave, that she should slay
Herself; and to the knight said, 'Yea,
Now that I know my father's will,
That in this manner I must kill

Myself, so be it: I shall do
Whatever he commands me to,
Because my choice cannot be other.
But I have something for my brother –
A letter which I shall compose
With feeble hand and heart of woes.'   270

She took her pen that he might learn
Of all the griefs which turn by turn
For her enduring were decreed.
She let her fatal lover read
How she might not, for anything,
Come by the mercy of the King;
And furthermore, as will appear,
She wrote these words, which thou shalt hear:
'O thou my sorrow and my calm,
O thou my sickness and my balm,   280
O all my hope and my despair,
Thou my desire, and thou my care;
O thou my weal, and thou my woe;
O thou my friend, and thou my foe;
O thou my love, and thou my hate:
For thy sake am I dedicate
To death, and may not pass it by.
And yet, with all my heart, while I
Have yet remaining any breath,
Thee shall I love until my death.   290
But if my little son should die,
One thing I pray: that he may lie
Beside me, buried in my grave.
And thus shalt thou remembrance have
Of both of us. For thou shalt see,
At this hour, how it is with me,
And how my trouble stands tonight:
Both tears and ink I use, to write
This letter, cold with grieving; and
I hold the pen in my right hand,   300

131

But in my left a sword; and on
My bosom lies and weeps my son,
Thy child and mine; and he sobs fast.
Now I am come unto my last:
Farewell; I perish. Think of me,
That thus I paid for loving thee.'

[*She falls upon the sword and dies. The pitiless King, her
father, exposes her child to the wild beasts of the forest. This
tale is followed by the story (from Ovid's* Metamorphoses,
*Book Three) of how Tiresias was changed into a woman because,
in anger, he smote two coupling snakes. Such are the tragedies of
melancholic wrath.*]

CONFESSOR:

The second sort of Wrath is Chiding.
Out like the storm-winds he goes riding,
And blows full many a sudden blast
Like theirs, and makes those folk aghast
Who only ask for peace and rest.
It is this same ungoodliest
Vice that splits many a loving heart;
His mouth is ever wide apart,
His lips unlocked, and all his thought
So fragmentary and distraught,
That everything which he can tell
Runs out like water from a well,
Spouts like a spring which cannot hide
The streams it pours on every side:
His bubbling gossip over-runs
In filth on his companions –
For sooner fill a sieve with ale
Than silence Chiding in his tale;
Too fast to hinder or oppose,
He will uncover all he knows.
As, at an unwalled city, men
May travel out and in again,
With neither let nor hindrance, so

His misbegotten wordy flow   440
Makes patent all he has within.
His hearers oftener lose than win;
For many a time, with heedless chidings,
He brings a household evil tidings
And stirs up war at the bed's head.
He is the leaven in the bread,
Which, being sour, sours all the dough.
He bears a ready-bended bow;
And, where he aims, the man is lost:
Beware of him at any cost,   450
And of the arrows of his tongue.
So loudly are his changes rung
That people, all the land around,
Cringe from the clamour of the sound
More than they do from that of thunder –
Which has less power to stir their wonder:
For such enormous winds he blows,
Time and again he overthrows
A city or a polity –
Whose folk, of high and low degree,   460
I have heard rail against their foe,
'Evil befall thee, tongue of woe!'

[*Gower protests that he is utterly guiltless of Chiding, in
matters of love, except insofar as he has often chided himself for
his own stupidity or carelessness. But, he says,*

All this has been of no avail,
However savagely I rail;
For 'owl mucks perch and perch mucks owl' –
And if a fellow will defoul
Himself, his profit you can guess:
It is not worth a leaf of cress.

Nevertheless, the Confessor tells him a few admonitory stories.]

CONFESSOR:

A man, my son, to buy him ease,

640 Must suffer as did Socrates,
Whose good example has been writ;
And thou shalt hear the truth of it.
The good example that I mean

Is nowadays not often seen
In human company; but he
Had *patience* of such high degree
That he could put it to the test
In something that was likeliest
To bring him pain: a shrewish wife
650 He wedded, and with trouble and strife
She drove away his peace completely.
Still softly he replied, and sweetly.
One day it chanced, as we are told,
In winter when the air was cold,
His wife had used the well to get
A pot of water, and had set
It down again within the house.
But then she saw her harmless spouse
Sit with his head stuck in a book,
660 Beside the fire, like one who took
A little comfort in his age.
Then she began to storm and rage
And ask him what the devil he thought
He meant by sitting doing naught
(Forsooth!) while she did all the work;
She said that husbands who would shirk
Were cheaper than a wisp of hay.
He answered neither nay nor yea,
But sat him still and let her chide.
670 But she, who would not be denied,
At once began to puff and swell:
What she had carried from the well,
The water-pot, she held aloft,
And bade him speak. But still and soft
He sat, and answered not a word.
Only for this, her anger stirred,

And she demanded, was he dead? –
And then poured out upon his head
The water, bidding him awaken.
But Socrates had not forsaken   680
His patience; he replied that she
Had done no harm that he could see,
But only what was natural:
For it was winter, after all;
And in the winter, as we know,
The storm winds cannot help but blow;
And when the winds have blown their fill
We have not long to wait until
The sky unbars its watergate:
'And so my wife at any rate,'   690
Said Socrates, 'has used her reason,
And done according to the season,
By sending me both wind and rain.'
And then beside the fire again
He sat until his clothes were dry.
Not one word more did he reply –
In which he acted for the best,
And earned himself a little rest.

[*Now follows the conclusion of the story of Tiresias, in which
he is punished with blindness. Next comes the tale of Phoebus
and Coronis, which may be found in Ovid,* Metamorphoses,
Book Two, and is given by Chaucer as the Manciple's Tale:
*the raven was once white, but was turned black for not keeping
counsel. Similarly, the nymph Lara was terribly punished for
betraying one of Jupiter's amours (Ovid,* Fasti, *ii: 585 ff.*).]

CONFESSOR:

My son, be thou like none of these,   831
With chatterings and calumnies;
Forbear to chide, especially,
For it is wisdom's enemy,
And wrathful speech is evil speech.

GOWER:

My father, everything you teach
Is very true; and as you school me,
So I shall do my best to rule me,
And flee from chiding: well betide
840   The man who has forborne to chide.
But now say on, if there is more
To learn of Wrath and all his lore.

[*The next form of Wrath is Hatred. Gower admits to having hated his Lady's cruel words, and those liars who baulk him in love. Otherwise he is guiltless. Nevertheless, he is told a warning tale – that of King Nauplius and the Greeks – which may be found in Benoît's* Roman de Troie.]

CONFESSOR:

973   After the ruin of Troy Town,
When it had all been beaten down,
And slain was Priamus the King,
The Greeks (who had caused everything)
Began to look towards home again.
Men struggle against Fate in vain;
We prove it, many a time and oft:
980   Hard weather follows after soft:
They took to sea; and as they went,
A tempest shook the firmament.
Then Hera bent her coloured bow,
The dark-sky winds went to and fro
Among a rage of fire and thunder
As though the world should split asunder;
Out from the heavens' watergate,
Rain was a torrent all in spate;
The tackle now went out of trim;
990   The men were helpless, rope and limb.
Now you might hear the shipmen cry
For fear that all of them must die –
And yet the steersman heard not them

Who shouted on the windy stem:
His ship reared up against the sea,
And a wild lodestone followed he.
The sea beat in on every side,
And no man knew what might betide;
They put in God their only trust,
To float or founder as they must.   1000

At this point, matters fell out thus:
A certain King called Nauplius,
Was father of an only son
Who led the Greeks at Ilion
Till he was Captain of them all.
(But fortune led him to his fall);
Prince Palamedes was his name,
And hate had caused the Greeks to aim
At compassing his death; and so
By treason came his overthrow.   1010
King Nauplius, having heard of it,
Swore that in time and season fit
He would see vengeance done for this –
And took an oath for emphasis.
And thus the King, with secret hate,
Bided his time and lay in wait:
He had not craft or chivalry
To take his vengeance openly.
Now rumour, which runs far and wide,
Brought news of how the Greeks had hied   1020
Them homeward out of Troy, and how
They were upon the ocean now.
At this, because King Nauplius knew
What the great ocean tides would do
When driven by a landward storm,
At once the King began to form
A plan whereby, through deep deceit,
To wreak his hatred on the fleet:
For well he knew, who could observe

137

1030 Such weather, that the fleet must swerve
Along his coastline in their flight.
So, in the darkness of the night,
With mighty timbers and with blocks,
He lit a fire above the rocks;
The cliffs threw back the enormous glare;
And the Greek navy saw it there.
Then all befell as he had planned:
Seeking the safety of the land,
They saw this beacon, far and bright
1040 And (thinking it some harbour light,
Lit only for their benefit,
Which, if they were to steer by it,
Would guide them in) they gladly steered
For it, the swifter as it neared.
There is great evil in deceit,
Men say; I prove it by this fleet:
For when they thought their haven found,
They struck upon the rocky ground
And shattered there by tens and twelves.
1050 The seamen could not help themselves;
There, where they thought they were secure,
Death came upon them doubly sure.
But though the vessels in the van
Were lost, when on the rocks they ran,
Yet they were able to apprise
The others, through both din and cries;
And, by the morning's early light,
These learned the secret of the night –
That, where they looked for friendly aid,
1060 Friendship and trust had been betrayed.
Then from that sea-coast where deceit
Had harmed them so, they swiftly beat
Away towards the open sea;
Nor was there one to disagree
That they must evermore beware
Of what they had experienced there.

[*Two further kinds of Wrath are known as Contest and Homicide. Gower has been guilty only of Contest in the heart, against his unkind fate. But even that, says his Confessor, is a sin. To point the moral (that Reason should contest all violence), he tells two quite familiar stories. First comes that of Alexander's visit to Diogenes. 'What do you want most?', asks Alexander. 'For you to move, and let me have a little sunlight in my barrel,' says Diogenes. There follows the story of Pyramus and Thisbe, a warning against over-hasty suicide, which Gower (and Chaucer in* The Legend of Good Women) *took from Ovid's* Metamorphoses, *Book Four. Thisbe's lament over the corpse of her lover is perhaps worth quoting.*]

[THISBE:]

'Thou, love's lord,   1462
Cupid by name, full well I find
That when thou guidest thou are blind;
Venus, protectress of love's laws,
Wast thou debarred, then, from this cause
Of grief between my love and me?
My Pyramus, whom here I see
Lie bleeding – was his death deserved?
You had he not obeyed and served?   1470
Was he not young, and am not I?
Alas, why use us so? And why,
When you had set our hearts on fire
With such a fashion of desire,
Give us no skill to make it truth?
The freshness of our joyful youth,
All joyless now, has pined away;
And this you never can repay.
Now, for myself, I say that I
Think it a dearer thing to die   1480
Than to out-live this woeful day.'

CONFESSOR:

And, having spoken thus, she lay

139

Beside her love, and him embraced,
And sought her own death in such haste
That – while she kissed and while she wept –
At last so deep a sorrow crept
Upon her spirit, unbeknown,
That she was wholly overthrown.
As in a dream, like one possessed,
1490 She set the sword-point to her breast,
And fell upon it; and before
That moment passed, she was no more.
There, dead and bloody from one blade,
The lover and his lass were laid.

My son, if you have understood
This tale, beware for thine own good
That foolish haste betrays thee not;
Use thy good sense, nor play the sot
By trusting luck to be thy friend:
1500 Thou art in peril to thine end,
So doing. If thou hast ere this
Erred thus, tell on and nothing miss.

GOWER:

My father, in what appertains
To love, my conscience *has* such stains:
When love has only brought me woe,
My spirit *has* been tempted so.
Had wishes power, upon my oath,
Often I had been nothing loth
To die a thousand times a day.
1510 For though indeed Love did not slay
Me outright, freely I confess
That my own will did little less.
My will is guilty, as you see:
And yet she will not pity me;
She holds my health and life in thrall,
But will not comfort me at all.

Full well I know whose fault it is;
And, if I could have, long ere this
I would have slain him – and shall still
Bear him in mind, to work him ill.   1520
Not all the gold of nine kings' lands
Should buy him from between my hands,
If he were at my mercy here;
And yet he holds me in no fear,
For all my threats. But it is he
Who keeps my Love away from me;
Nor, till he dies, may I succeed.
What can I do, then, but take heed
Of means for putting him away?
And I shall use what means I may.   1530

CONFESSOR:

Tell me, my son, in verity,
Who is this mortal enemy
Whose threatened death is all thy thought?

GOWER:

A villain and a thing of naught!
Wherever I come, he comes there first
And sees to it my cause is cursed.

CONFESSOR:

His name, then?

GOWER:

          Danger.* What is more,
He is my lady's counsellor:
Nor have I ever managed yet,
By any cunning ruse, to get   1540
Close to my Love, but night or day,
Danger was there to say me nay

* See note in Book One, l. 2443 (p. 87).

And see that I should never reach
My Love, for guerdon or for speech.
My father, this is ever true:
All that my Love would say or do
To me, this Danger will deny,
And so turns all my world awry.
When asked for help, he is the same,
1550 And still *Sanz Pité** is his name:
The more I beg, and bend my knee,
The less he will attend to me.
He keeps my love so gulled and tied,
She will not let him leave her side;
Thus he hangs round her – and has brought
Himself so privy to her thought
That, if I have a boon to pray,
I still find Danger in the way:
His voice will answer, never hers –
1560 And, for all boons that *he* confers,
I might as well have held my tongue.
Such evil answers he has flung
At me, that worse there could not be.
Between this Danger, then, and me,
Is bitter war until he dies.
But could I compass or devise
Danger to vanquish or destroy,
That were the sunrise of my joy:
I would not stray aside for sin
1570 Though all the world were mine to win;
Oh for some engine – my estate
In balance for a counterweight –
With which, by skill, I might dissever
Him from my Lady's Court forever!

[*All his wishes are vain, however. The Confessor counsels him
to possess his soul in patience, because 'more haste, less speed':
For, men say, he who runs will rue;*
    * i.e. *sans pitié* – 'merciless'.

And alewives, careless of the brew,
May well repent it when they drink.
Better it is to swim than sink;
Better upon the bridle chew
Than, if by hasting, the horse threw
His man, and foundered in the mire. . . .

Moreover, 'how can the mouse compel the cat?' Endure all
things, and avoid foolish haste – in illustration of which Vice,
the Confessor tells two stories. The first, from Ovid's Meta-
morphoses, Book One, *is that of Phoebus and his amorous*
pursuit of Daphne, who escaped by being changed into a laurel.
The second, from Benoît's Roman de Troie, *is that of*
Athemas and Demophon. After the fall of Troy, returning to
their kingdoms, they found their peoples recalcitrant. But
instead of resorting to force and battle, they won over the rebels
by fair speech. In love, do nothing hastily, nothing by force.
The Confessor now turns to Homicidal Violence, and tells
the story of Orestes. This is, essentially, the familiar classical
story, though Gower appears to have taken it also from Benoît.]

CONFESSOR:

Of this example, take good heed:
In love, whomever would succeed
By murder, all the world will blame,
And put him and his love to shame.   2200

GOWER:

My father, their unhappy fate
Would leave my heart disconsolate,
I do assure you, were I not
So eager to learn what is what,
And all I should or should not do.
But one boon more I ask of you:
Now, by your leave, tell me, I pray,
If there be any lawful way
To slay a man, and not transgress.

CONFESSOR:

2210 My son, in several cases, yes.
Those guilty of a robbery,
Of murder, or of treachery,*
Such men the judge must not forgive;
His duty says they shall not live;
To waver is a deadly sin:
For he with law and justice in
His hands, who wields it not, but spares,
Betrays the office which he bears:
For when he pours his mercy out
2220 Upon a single rogue, no doubt
A thousand good men come to grief.
Such mercy may, in his belief,
Please God; but there he deviates,
Unless all Reason abdicates.
The law said, long ere we were born,
That Swords of Kingship should be worn
As emblems that a king protects
His loyal people, and subjects
All such as mean them ill. Therefore,
2230 My son, in justice to restore
The laws, and common weal to win,
A man may kill and do no sin,
But rather be to praise and bless
For thus maintaining righteousness.
And further: for his country's sake,
In time of war, a man shall make
His own defence of house and land
(And of himself) with his own hand;
And, as the law stands, he shall slay
2240 If he can find no better way.

GOWER:

Then, father, my next question is
Of them whose bloody business

* i.e. treason in the modern sense.

Is deadly war for worldly cause:
Can such men slay within the laws?

CONFESSOR:

Upon thy question, good my son,
Thou shalt hear my opinion,
Within the compass of my wit,
As God's clear laws occasion it:
All I know of it, I shall tell,
To help thee rule thy conscience well.   2250

The Lord of Righteousness on high
(As the Commandments testify)
Forbids that horrid sin to us –
Murder most foul and villainous.
And when His Son was born, He sent
Down angels, through the firmament,
Whose song of peace the shepherds heard:
'Peace upon earth' (this was their word)
'Among all people of good will.'
And so, upon this question still,   2260
If charity be held in awe,
Then deadly wars offend its law:
Such wars make war on Nature too;
Peace is the end her laws pursue –
Peace, the chief gem in Adam's wealth;
Peace which is all his life and health.
But in the gangs of war there go
Poverty, pestilence, and woe,
And famine, and all other pain
Whereof we mortal men complain,   2270
Whom war shall trample down until
Our only succour is God's will.
For it is war that brings to naught,
On Earth, all good that God has wrought:
The church is burnt, the priest is slain;
Virgin and wife, vile rapes constrain;

Law pines away, God is not served:
Now tell me, what has he deserved,
The man who brings such warfare in?
2280 First, if he stirred up war to win
Advantage, count his heavy cost,
With all the people who are lost:
By any worldly reckoning,
The man has not won anything.
Then, if he acts in hope of grace
From heaven, it is not my place
To speak of such rewards; but still,
Both love and peace were Our Lord's will;
And he who works their opposite
2290 Must reap an ill reward from it.
Since in their nature, as we find,
Battles and wars of every kind
Are so displeasing to Our Lord,
And since their temporal reward
Is woe, it mystifies the mind
To guess at what can ail mankind
That they agree no armistice:
Sin, I think, is what makes us miss;
And sin is paid with death. I know
2300 Not how such matters truly go;
But as for us, who are of one
Belief, in my opinion
Peace were a better thing to choose
Than ways by which we doubly lose.

[*The true cause of war, says the Confessor, is covetousness.
This truth is well exemplified in the wars of Greece and Persia;
but Arcady was so poor a district that it was left in peace.
And so today: rich or poor, men go to war for land, for spoil,
or for pay. There follows the story of King Alexander and the
Pirate, which may be found in St Augustine, in the* Gesta
Romanorum, *and elsewhere. A Pirate was arraigned before
Alexander, and justified himself by saying that he was only*

146

doing on a small scale what Alexander did imperially. Never-
theless, Alexander himself at last came to a tragic end. So let
us not slaughter men unless in the cause of justice.]

GOWER:

My father, I have understood   2485
All you have said; but fain I would
Have one more answer, yes or no:
Is it the law that men may go
Across the Middle Sea to fight
And slay the Saracen?

CONFESSOR:

        I cite   2490
The Gospel, son, wherein I read
That men may preach and men may bleed
For Holy Faith; I find not 'slay'.
That Christ, with His own death, should pay
For all of us, and set us free,
Is token of pure charity;
And having taught, and being dead,
He sent Apostles in His stead –
Twelve who should go the world around
And preach the Faith on foreign ground   2500
(Whereby, in each his destined place,
They died); and so, by Heaven's grace,
The Faith of Christ had strength to rise:
But if they had done otherwise,
And made it an excuse to kill,
The faith had been uncertain still.

[*All slaying, then, is evil. To prove this, the Confessor tells*
how Peleus slew his brother Phocus, and how Alcmaeon killed
his own mother. Homicide can make men worse than wild
beasts and birds of prey.]

CONFESSOR:

Solinus'* book describes, I find,

   * Gower is mistaken: this account is *not* in Solinus.

147

2600 A creature of a wondrous kind:
Among the birds, one sort is known
That has a face of flesh and bone,
Like to a man's in every way.
This creature is a bird of prey;
And when it finds one, if it can,
The bird will kill and eat a man;
Then, having gorged, forthwith it will
Go to a fountain or a rill;
And, bending down to take its drink,
2610 Will see its mirrored face, and think
How this is – one might say – the twin
Of the dead man's. And then its sin
Lies heavy on the bird; the force
Of conscience breeds in it remorse
So bitter that for very sorrow
It cannot live until the morrow.
From this example we conclude
That homicide must be eschewed:
For mercy's way is ever good,
2620 So laws be kept and understood,
Nor justice lead the other way.
For often I have heard men say,
Men in the middle of a war,
That sometimes they made conquests more
By sparing than by slaying men,
And were not sorry for it then.

[*This point is illustrated by the tale of Achilles and Teuthras, King of Mysia. About to slay King Teuthras, Achilles was dissuaded by Telephus. Nevertheless, the Greeks won the battle; and, later, Telephus was made heir to the Kingdom. (This tale also comes from Benoît.) The Confessor now sums up: patience and mercy are the cures for every form of Wrath. He now introduces the next of the sins, which is Sloth.*]

Book Four: Sloth

CONFESSOR:

THE first degree of Sloth I call
Delay – and he is worst of all,
Because his nature is the kind
That lets all business get behind.
What he might finish now and here
Will linger on throughout the year
With his, 'Tomorrow; yes, tomorrow.'
So long as there is Time to borrow,   10
He thinks God will provide and lend;
And when he means to make an end,
He is least likely to begin.
Now, this brings many a mischief in
Upon him, unbeknown: at last
The chance to save him has gone past.
The lineaments of laziness
In Love are neither more nor less:
His inactivity today
May throw his final chance away.   20
My son, in matters of this kind,
Hast thou no guilt upon thy mind –
As touching love – of laziness?
If so, speak on.

GOWER:

Good father, yes.
Delay may count me as his own;
I wear his livery, am shown
In the front rank of all his suite:
For, though resolving to compete
For her, and having set a day
To speak to the dear girl, Delay   30

Has said, 'More sensible to wait;
The time is not appropriate
For speaking to her yet.' And so,
With all his whisperings to and fro,
He steals my time away from me;
For, when no fairer chance could be,
He says, 'Another day were better;
Wiser, perhaps, to send a letter
Lest, in her presence, you should fear
40   To be entirely frank and clear?'
Thus I have let my chances slide;
My sloth has lost me time and tide;
Sinful delays have come of it,
And often so befooled my wit
(And all I meant to do or say
Has been so tangled in delay)
That in the end my chance was gone.
I know not what my mind was on,
Nor whether I felt fear or shame;
50   But, ever in earnest or in game,
I know how long a time has passed.
Yet the great love stands firm and fast
As ever, towards my lady: though
My tongue, in begging, may be slow
At all times, yet, as I have prayed,
This heart of mind has never strayed
From busily beseeching grace –
Which I may not as yet embrace.
And God knows, this is *malgré moi**
60   For I at least am sure, *ma foi*,
So rarely does that grace appear,
Its is a tardiness I fear
More than all others I have met
Within the Court of Love as yet.

---

* Gower has 'malgre myn' and 'a fin', respectively, instead of
the French phrases given by me.

[There follows the familiar story of Dido and Aeneas, and of how she died because he delayed his return. Next is the tale, based upon a passage in Ovid's Heroic *Epistles, of how Ulysses at last hastened home to Penelope: this does not, however, take the* Odyssey *into account. Last of the tales about Delay is a legend of uncertain origin: that of Robert Grosteste. For seven years, by secret arts, Grosteste laboured to forge a brazen head that should foretell the future. One moment of inattention, and his labours were lost. Think also, says the Confessor, of the five foolish virgins; and beware of idleness in love. Now, there is a second form of Sloth: Pusillanimity – which means lack of heart to undertake the duty of a man.]*

CONFESSOR:

And so, my son, if we begin   340
To speak of love and of Love's Court,
There too are shirkers of that sort –
Men who lack heart when it were best
That love were (but for fear) confessed;
But they are dumb, and dare not tell,
And stand as mute as any bell –
Its clapper gone – that cannot chime:
So they swing helpless for a time,
Spiritless and bereft of speech,
Without the courage to beseech . . .   350

[Gower confesses to this vice, and is told the Story of Pygmalion and his Statue, from Metamorphoses, *Book Ten.]*

CONFESSOR:

Never was fairer statue yet;   381
And it was easy to forget
She did not live: from ivory white
He wrought her, and for more delight
Stained her with rose upon the cheeks
And lips, and half believes she speaks.
So tenderly the red mouth smiled,

Even Pygmalion was beguiled:
And his imagination wrought
390   Upon him so, his deepest thought
And inmost heart of love were laid
On this fair image he had made;
But when he spoke his love, she could
Not answer, and still silent stood.
All day, whatever he might do,
He had the statue by him too:
And, even when he sat at meat,
Would serve her, coaxing her to eat,
Or lifting to her lips a cup.
400   And when the plates were taken up,
Would bring her to his private room
Where in the quiet and the gloom
He stretched her naked in his bed.
What weary vigils, what tears shed,
In kissing her cold mouth so oft,
And wishing that its lips were soft!
Often he whispered in her ear,
Caressed her body everywhere,
Or drew her into his embrace;
410   And evermore he begged for grace,
As if the stone could have consented.
Thus by himself was he tormented
In such an anguish of desire,
None else could bring him pain so dire.
And yet it happened that he prayed
So hard, and in this penance stayed
So faithfully, both day and night,
That Venus, pitying his plight,
One midnight granted him his prayer;
420   For then, when he could hardly bear
His pain, upon his naked arm
He felt the cold stone growing warm:
And there lay flesh and blood, and life.
Thus did he win a lusty wife

Able and ready to his will.
Had he done nothing, but sat still,
In silence, all his hope had failed;
But his persistent prayers availed:
Because he spoke, his love was sped.
All he desired, he found abed: 430
They were not severed in their joy

Ere the begetting of a boy
(Paphus was afterwards the name
They gave him; and it is the same
As that of the Greek island styled
Paphos from him who was their child).

[*Another singular story, adds the Confessor, is to the same
point. (It is based upon Ovid's* Metamorphoses, *Book Nine.*)]

CONFESSOR:

King Ligdus, in a private strife   451
With Telethusa, his queen-wife
(She being pregnant then), had sworn
That if a girl-child should be born
It should be suffered in no wise
To live; for, 'Soon as born, it dies,'
He said: and she was very grieved.
Her womb would shortly be relieved;
And it befell that, in this plight,
Isis came secretly by night –   460
As goddess of all parturition –
To help her in her sad condition.
Soon she was slender as before:
Yet it had been a girl she bore.
The goddess bade her, none the less,
Preserve the child, and not confess:
Iphis, a boy's name, they supplied;
And thus the King was satisfied.
In her own chamber, then, the Queen
Kept the child close to her, unseen;   470

153

But brought her up in every way –
In clothing, and in all array –
Like any boy of royal blood.
And that is how the matter stood
Till Iphis reached the age of ten;
He was betrothed in marriage then
To a Duke's daughter, and soon wed
To this Ianthe. Oft in bed,
These children (for their years agree)
480 Have lain together, she and she,
Mere playfellows in innocence.
But no more than a few years thence,
When they were both abed one night,
Nature – whose laws may well incite
All creatures upon earth to muse –
So works upon them that they use
Employments quite beyond their ken.
Cupid took pity on them then,
And on their deep frustrated passion,
490 And ordered matters in such fashion
That their desires grew natural,
And his laws triumphed after all
(For there is nothing Love hates more
Than what runs counter to the lore
That Nature plants in human kind).
The God of Love, then, so designed
His mercy, in the present case,
That Nature entered their embrace:
For when the time seemed fittest, when
500 These two were closely kissing, then
Iphis was turned into a man –
Whereby true wedded love began
With young Ianthe, his fair wife;
Thus they could live a happy life,
And Nature suffer no offence.

Take this, my son, as evidence

That Love will evermore be kind
To them, that, with a steadfast mind,
Continue eager to pursue
Those rituals which are his due.   510

[*And so to the next form of Sloth or Accidia. This is called
Forgetfulness, and can make a lover omit two-thirds of what he
had intended to say to his lady. Gower has been guilty of this,
for he is afraid of his lady:*
        And like a man who suddenly
        Beholds a spectre, so fare I:
        For very fear, I cannot set
        My wits in order, but forget
        Even myself and why I came. . . .
        My speech and hearing come to grief;
        I am not worth an ivy-leaf.
*All this is foolish, for his lady gives no cause for alarm;
and Gower often reproaches himself for his folly and forget-
fulness. On the other hand, sometimes his joy in her company has
the same effect. All this will never do, says the Confessor –
'Gird up your heart for busy-ness' – and he tells Gower the
story of Demophon and Phyllis, a version of which may be
found in Chaucer's* Legend of Good Women. *Ovid is the
principal source.*]

CONFESSOR:

By ship to Troy, King Demophon   731
And all his company were gone.
It chanced that on the voyage, he
Put in awhile at Rhodope
(For Aeolus had blown him there)
For a short rest and for repair.
It chanced that, while he tarried thus,
The daughter of Ligurgius* –
Who reigned in Rhodope as Queen –
Had for a certain season been   740
In her town fortress near the strand

* Thus Gower; but the real name of the father was Sithon.

Where Demophon had come to land.
Her name was Phyllis; young in years,
In her, both face and form, appears
Nothing that could be lovelier.
Now, Demophon attracted her;
So, when he joined her, she made much
Of him; his character was such,
This lusty knight, he could but learn
To love the lady in return.
And thus, within a day or so,
He thought, 'However things may go,
At least I mean to try my chance.'
With sweet words, he began to advance
His suit; and, whispering in her ear,
At last he quietened her fear:
For this, he swore, was his troth-plight
Ever to be her own true knight.
And thus together they abode,
While still the ships at anchor rode;
And they had ample time and space
To speak of love and learn its grace.
She trusted all he had to say:
When he would vow, when he would pray,
All this – to her – was ravishment,
For she was but an innocent.
She took his words as Gospel truth,
Thought him sincere in very sooth,
And – more the pity that she should –
Granted her lover all he would.
And thus he had no little joy
Till the hour came to go to Troy.
Great was her grief and sorrow then;
But he had sworn to come again –
'If I am living and I may' –
A month from his departing-day.
Many the kisses from them both;
But, were they fain or were they loth,

To ship he must; and so he went
To Troy, as was his first intent.   780
The days run on, the month goes by;
Her loves increase, and his loves die.
From sleep or food she turns away;
But Demophon forgets his day.
At last the sorrowful young queen,
Who cannot guess what this must mean,
Writes to him, begging him return:
The powers of love within her burn
So fiercely that she thinks it sure
She cannot very long endure   790
To live apart from Demophon.
She bids his conscience dwell upon
The oaths of true love that he swore,
And how she gave herself therefor;
She says, if he should still delay
Beyond a certain trysting-day,
She will have perished of his sloth –
And shame, then, on his plighted troth!
Forth on its way this letter sped,
And she was somewhat comforted;   800
For she had only to await
Her lover's coming, on the date
That she had written to propose.
Pity it is to tell, God knows;
But still he tarried, and forgot
His day once more, and so came not.
But she remembered well; she eyed
The calendar, for meeting-tide,
And cast her gaze across the sea:
It was, and then it was not, he;   810
'It is his ship; no, it is naught':
Thus did she waver in her thought,
And knew not what to think or say.
But fasting all the livelong day,
Into the watches of the night,

157

She sets a lantern with a light
High on the summit of a tower;
And thither climbs she, every hour,
To keep it burning clear and plain
820   And light her lover home again:
Seeing far off that harbour-light,
Then he could steer to her by night.
All was mistaken, all in vain;
For Venus dashed her hopes again
And, shining, showed her from the sky
That early morning was hard by
And that the light of risen day
Could not be very far away.
Then she beheld the sea at large;
830   And, seeing neither ship nor barge,
As far as human eye could scan,
Down from the tower-top she ran
Into an arbour, all alone;
And there she made most bitter moan,
Unheard by any living thing.
For life had no more joy to bring;
And now she swooned, and now complained;
Her lovely countenance was stained
With streaming floods of tears that fell
840   Down from her eyes as from a well.
There also, ever and anon,
She called the name of Demophon:
'Alas, thou slow and tardy wight!
When was there ever such a knight
For sloth and cold forgetfulness,
Or like thee for ungentleness,*
Who broke the word that he had given?'
Then, casting up her eyes to heaven,
She said, 'O thou untrue, unkind,
850   Here shalt thou in thy slowness find,

* Discourtesy.

158

If thou shouldst please to come and see,
A lady dead for love of thee;
For in this place I mean to die –
I whom thou wouldst not comfort, I
Whom thou mightst well have saved ere now.'
So saying, to a leafy bough
She knotted fast the belt of silk
That she had worn; then, white as milk,
Her neck received the other knot;
And she hung dead upon the spot.   860
At this the Gods were deeply moved,
And Demophon himself reproved;
For now appeared, at their command,
A witness that should ever stand
Against forgetfulness and sloth:
Lo, Phyllis was transformed, by growth
Into a new nut-bearing tree
For all the world of men to see;
And Phyllis' name was given it
In orchards where it grew, to wit   870
The Filbert: to her lover's shame,
Unto this day, it bears that name.

[*Beware, then, of Forgetful Sloth. Now, there is another kind of
Sloth, and that is Negligence. Negligence puts off everything
until it is too late; then he says, 'If only I had known!'*
    And when he finds his finest steed
    Is stolen, then he will take heed
    And double-lock the stable door.
*Gower denies that he has been this kind of lover. Nevertheless,
he is told the stories of Phaeton and of Icarus, which are both
based upon tales in Ovid's Metamorphoses. The former is a
warning against aiming too low in love, by neglecting its higher
aspects; the latter, against aiming too high, and leaving one's
duties undone. And thus we come to the next form of Sloth,
which is Idleness.*]

CONFESSOR:

Now, he seeks comforts manifold:
1090 In winter, never stirs for cold
(In summer, heat will be his let);
So, whether his body freeze or sweat,
Or be he in, or be he out,
We see him idling all about –
Unless he plays at dice a little.
For he will take no jot or tittle
Of wages honour may deserve,
From any lord whom he might serve
As one among his retinue,
1100 Unless perchance he holds in view
Some means whereby, through some pretence,
Or sheltered under eminence,
He can the better dawdle still,
And be as idle as he will.
He finds it troublesome to take
A journey for his lady's sake,
But feeds himself upon his wishes;
So, like a cat which longs for fishes,
But will not get his talons wet,
1110 So Idleness lives on – and yet
Can seldom win to his desire.
Son, wast thou forged in such a fire?
Tell on, and plainly speak thy shrift.

GOWER:

Father, this vow to God I lift:
That in Love's service I have never,
I think, been idle; nor shall ever,
While I have any strength, be so.

CONFESSOR:

Then, good my son, now let me know
What labours thou dost undertake

For Love and for thy lady's sake,   1120
So full of honour as she is.

GOWER:

My father, all my life till this,
In every place, whatever she
At any time has bidden me,
That I have done with diligence
And with heartfelt obedience.
And if she will command me naught,
I do what first comes to my thought
As being in my power; so
I offer service, bowing low,   1130
Whether in chamber or in hall,
As opportunity may fall.
When she is going to hear Mass,
Few are the moments I let pass
Before I meet my love and say
I will assist her on her way
To chapel, and then home again.
Nor do I count my labour vain:
It is not nothing that I win
When I, who may not stroke her skin,   1140
Have led her, clothed, upon my arm –
Though afterwards it does me harm,
Because of my imagination:
This is the kind of thought I fashion
Within me, many a time and oft:
'Oh Lord, how rounded and how soft
She is; how slender and how small!
Now would to God I had her all
For mine, compliant to my will!'
Then I sigh deeply – and sit still,   1150
Because I know my fevered thought
Is idle, and will come to naught.
But for all that, another day,
I do whatever good I may;

My eagerness is none the less,
To serve my lady's worthiness.
Then how I burnish all my wit,
To recognize occasions fit,
And what I should or should not do!
1160 At last, if she permits me to,
I carry out her least intent;
I go at once where I am sent,
Come when it pleases her to call:
And thus my Love has conquered all
My lethargy, until I die;
Serve her I must, no choice have I;
For, as men say, need knows no law:
Nearer I cannot help but draw,
To look, to serve, to bow to the ground;
1170 My glances follow her around;
Whatever *she* wants, so do I:
When she sits down, I kneel close by;
And when she rises, I will stand.
Then, if she has some work on hand,
As weaving or embroidery,
What can I do but muse, to see
Fingers so long and delicate?
And now I think, and now I prate,
And now I sigh, and now I sing,
1180 As an excuse for tarrying.
But if she finds that for a while
My company does not beguile,
And turns to other business,
I have devices none the less
To drag along the weary day –
For I am loth to go away.
So then I act the simple sort
Of man whose pleasure is to sport –
Or feign to – with her little hound
1190 Upon the bed or on the ground,
Or with her songbirds in their cage.

Why, even with her smallest page
Or with her humblest chambermaid,
I have been pleasant, or have played,
In hope they might speak well of me.
My round is busy, as you see;
I do not idly hang about!
Now, if she wishes to go out
On pilgrimage or pleasure-ride,
Unbidden I am by her side   1200
To lift her in my arms aloft
And set her in the saddle soft,
And lead her palfrey by the bridle:
And all for fear of being idle.
But if – and if I am aware –
She rides by coach to take the air,
I too prepare myself to ride
Close by her, at the carriage side. . . .

[*And so forth. The Confessor readily acquits Gower of
Idleness in Love. Nevertheless, he tells the story of Rosiphile,
Princess of Armenia – which is in the main original. Although
she was wise and beautiful, she was cold and slow in love,
desiring neither paramours nor marriage. Venus and Cupid
resolved, therefore, to punish her, and so change her disposi-
tion.*]

CONFESSOR:

It happened, in the month of May,   1283
Before the dawning of the day,
That she desired to walk, unknown
Save to her women, all alone,
And else unseen by mortal eye,
Into her park, which lay nearby.
Softly along the grass she strayed
Until she came upon a glade   1290
And, running through it broad and clear,
A river. Said the Princess, 'Here

I shall abide within the shaw.'
She bade her women to withdraw,
And there she stood alone and still
Until she had resolved her will.
She saw the fragrant flowers springing;
She heard the happy songbirds singing;
She saw the beasts of every kind,
1300 The buck, the doe, the hart, the hind,
Go male with female; and within
She felt a kind of war begin,
Cupid contending with her heart,
Disquiet which would not depart.
And, as she cast her eyes about,
Riding towards her came a rout
Of ladies, in one livery,
Beside the wood, in company;
And every gently ambling steed
1310 Was white and tall, and stout indeed,
Pacing the woodland in a row.
Their saddles made a splendid show –
So thick-adorned with pearl and gold,
No man might richer work behold.
The ladies all wore one design
Of cope and kirtle, rich and fine,
And parti-coloured blue and white;
And with all manner of delight
These were embroidered everywhere.
1320 Slender and tall their bodies were;
And the fey* beauty on each face
No earthly power might debase.
On every head a crown was seen,
As if each lady were a queen;
Nor all the gold in Croesus' hall,
Paid for the meanest coronal,

---

* The texts read, variously, 'faye' and 'faire'. 'Faye', strictly, means *fairy*; but I have allowed myself the licence of the more expressive word.

Had truly given worth for worth.
And thus the company rode forth.
For very shame, when this she spied,
The Princess drew herself aside,   1330
Under the boughs; and, still and shy,
Lay hid until they passed her by.

[*At length Rosiphile sees one lady, in the rear of the company,
riding upon a* black *horse with only a white star upon its
forehead. It is in a miserable condition, and so are its trappings,
apart from a sumptuous bridle. The lady too is shabby, and
round her waist she wears a great horse-halter. Questioned by
Rosiphile, this lady discloses that her companions are true
servants of Love, while she herself is being punished – degraded
from a princess to a mere ostler – for sloth in love. But her
bridle at least is rich, as a reward for her one brief love affair.
So saying, she vanishes; and Rosiphile resolves to mend her
ways. Men and maidens, the Confessor says, should all make
haste to love and wed; and he proves it by the tale of Jephthah's
daughter (Judges xi), who died a virgin. Furthermore, men
who are lovers should prove their manhood in foreign battles, or
crusades, so that their lady may admire them. Gower con-
fesses that he has never done such a thing; if he left his lady, he
would be afraid of losing her:*

> ... It were a mockery of gain,
> To win the chaff and lose the grain.

*Were it not better if churchmen fulfilled their missionary
purpose, rather than idling at home? Perhaps, the Confessor
admits; but patience is a virtue. And he tells the story of
Ulysses and King Nauplius. This recounts how Ulysses pretend-
ed madness (by yoking foxes to a plough, and sowing the
furrows with salt) in order not to join the Trojan campaign;
but he was afterwards recalled by Nauplius to duty and honour.
One should bear in mind also the examples of Protesilaus (who
died with honour rather than live prudently), of Saul (I Samuel
xxviii), and of Achilles, who was trained up to combat, and
came to surpass all other knights. Then, too, there are the*

cases of Aeneas, of Lancelot, and of Hercules (who won his wife by prowess, and even inspired Queen Penthesilea to emulate him), and of Philemenis.]

CONFESSOR:

2191　So now, my son, as I have told
　　　And thou mayst see, he who is bold,
　　　Daring, and strenuous, and will make
　　　Himself Love's champion, he shall take
　　　The greatest share of ladies' grace:
　　　Women, if they are worthy, place
　　　Their love and trust in worthiness
　　　Of manhood and of *gentilesse*:*
　　　And gentle men are most desired.

GOWER:

2200　Father, unless I be inspired
　　　By you to learn, I cannot know
　　　What *gentilesse* may mean; and so,
　　　I beg, explain the word to me.

CONFESSOR:

　　　In common usage we may see
　　　Clearly, my son, within what ground
　　　A definition may be found:
　　　The name of *gentilesse* adheres
　　　To those who have for many years
　　　Been blessed with wealth and increment;
2210　But men of long and high descent
　　　May well be gentle in their name
　　　Alone, and have no real claim.
　　　All reasonable men admit
　　　That wealth is not the root of it,
　　　For wealth may often melt away;

---

* Like 'gentle' (l. 2211 etc.) this word implies courtesy, integrity, good breeding, as well as – and in preference to – what is involved in the modern 'gentlefolk' or 'gentry'.

The magnate in whose home today
Are all the riches of the Earth,
Tomorrow finds himself in dearth,
His riches gone upon the hour.
In riches, then, there is no power   2220
By which the name is justified.
Now view it from another side:
Does *gentilesse* proceed from birth?
Adam was first of men on Earth,
And Eve his wife, of women: then
All men on Earth were gentle men.
So *gentilesse* does not proceed
From high antiquity of breed,
And that resolves our question; for
The reason, as we see once more,   2230
Is that antiquity of birth
Is common to all men on Earth,
In equal measure and degree.
Be a man poor or wealthy, he
Came from his mother's womb unclad;
And in that hour the noble had
No richer cloth or covering
Than had the poorest beggarling.
And when they both shall die, who can
Declare which is the poorer man   2240
In worldly goods? But this I say,
The noble will have more to pay
When God has reckoned what they owe:
He had his pleasures here below.
As for the mortal flesh of man,
Though there be many roads which can
Lead him to death, they have one end;
And thither every man must wend,
The beggar lying by the lord,
All differences now ignored: 2250
The earth, which is our grandmother,
Receives alike both one and t'other;

She swallows back into her womb,
Impartially, no matter whom.
Thus I am very sure indeed
No *gentilesse* derives from breed.
There is no virtue without grace;
And whereas wealth and pride of place,
Oft when a person thinks he stands
2260   Secure, may slip from out his hands,
No wild or cruel fortune may
Uproot or cause to fade away
True virtue planted in the heart,
Until the soul and body part:
And then its guerdon shall be great
And evermore inviolate.
May it not well be *gentilesse*
That has such power to save and bless?
It is the nature and condition
2270   Of human reason and cognition –
Which offspring of the soul suffice
To tell a virtue from a vice,
And help men turn, this understood,
From vice and sloth, and follow good –
It is from these that men obtain
Their *gentilesse*: all else is vain,
All wealth or power they possess.
Today the truth is, none the less,
That in Love's Court it is decreed
2280   That humble virtue may not speed
When wealthy vice comes there to woo:
Love will not often have to do
With gentle folk in penury,
For all their noble courtesy.
But if both blessings light on men,
If they have wealth *and* virtue, then
They are most fortunate indeed.
Yet still, if they are to succeed,
They cannot afford Idleness;

2290   For neither wealth nor *gentilesse*
    Can help a man who will not toil.

[*Now follows a passage in praise of the twin virtues of love
and labour – both manual and mental. The discoverers and
inventors of many arts and sciences are commemorated; then the
Confessor embarks upon a long digression about Alchemy and
the discoveries of the 'Philosophers' in transforming and in-
creasing metals. The bases of Alchemy are seven Bodies and
four Spirits. These Bodies derive from the planets:* Gold
springs from the sun, Silver from the Moon, Iron from Mars,
Lead from Saturn, Brass from Jupiter, Copper from Venus.
Quicksilver belongs to Mercury, and is also the first of the
Spirits, of which the other three are Sal Ammoniac, Sulphur,
and Arsenic. Gold and silver are held to be noble metals, to
which the others are related and to which the baser metals
can be transformed by purification. This is a sevenfold process –
demanding great care in distillation, congelation, solution,
descension, sublimation, calcination, and fixation – which will
at last produce the perfect Elixir or Philosophers' Stone.
There are, however, three such stones. The first is called Lapis
Vegetabilis, which preserves the body from sickness; the
second, Lapis Animalis, which preserves and sharpens the
five senses; the third is called Mineral, and is that which
refines all other metals into gold and silver. Unhappily, the
art of making these stones has been lost: many are diligent in
their researches, but*

      Some hindrance always, or some let,
      There is; and poverty and debt
      Befall them who were rich before;
      Lucre they lose, for all their lore;
      To get a pound, they squander five:
      How can a craft of this sort thrive?

*After a list of early Alchemists, the Confessor turns to men
who were active in literature and languages – and, above*

---

* By this must be understood, of course, 'planets' in the medieval
sense: i.e. Sun, Moon, Saturn, Mars, Jupiter, Venus, Mercury.

all, praises Ovid for his learning in the subject of Love.
And so at last he introduces the last but one of the modes
of Sloth. This is Somnolence.]

CONFESSOR:

2705 And he is Sloth's own chamberlain,
Who scores of times could not refrain
From sleep when duty bade him wake.
With Love he had this truce to make;
'Let any waken if he will;
2710 As long as I may couch my fill,
Then I will seek no other tryst.'
He often goes to bed unkissed,
And says no wanton dalliance
Shall stir him from that sluggish trance.
And though true men would not concur,
Sleep makes his nature happier
Than wooing. Often, then, at night,
When lusty lords take their delight
Among the ladies, he will stare
2720 And skulk away like any hare
And go to bed; and, lying soft,
Dreams of his indolence full oft:
Of being glued into the mire;
Of sitting idly by the fire
And scratching at his naked shanks;
Of how he climbs up weary banks
To slide into some hollow dell.
If one were there to mark him well –
When he is lost in such a dream –
2730 Like ships that strain against the stream
He snores; a slumbrous noise he makes,
And sputters like a friar's cakes
When they are dropped into the fat.
Then also, it is rarely that
This fellow dreams of lusty things;
But when he does, all heaven sings

Within him, all the world is his:
And when he wakes he gives of this
A long and ordered explanation –
Of exploits that have no foundation.   2740
And it is thus, and only thus,
In love, that he is duteous.
What thanks can such a man deserve?
But thou, son, if thou thinkst to serve
The Court of Love, shouldst not act so.

GOWER:

Assuredly, good father, no!
I had much rather, by my troth,
(Than live a life so full of sloth
And wear a face that looks for bed),
Lose both mine eyes out of my head.   2750

[*And so on, for many lines of elaborate denial, and of precise
description of his wakefulness. His loving service keeps him
wakeful by day, his longing by night. When at last he does
sleep, he is tormented by amorous or despairing dreams. Father
Genius seizes upon this point, and tells the story of King Ceyx
and Halcyone his wife. This is from Ovid's* Metamorphoses,
*Book Eleven. Ceyx had a brother named Daedalion, who had
been transformed into a goshawk. The King sailed away on a
pilgrimage, to see if his brother might be restored to human
shape, and left his wife behind. He did not return within the
expected two months, and so Halcyone prayed to Juno for
information about him. Juno dispatched Iris, her messenger, to
visit Halcyone in a dream.*]

CONFESSOR:

This Iris, from the lofty floor
Of heaven, must be ambassador.
She donned her showery mantle, full
Of colours the most wonderful   2980
And varied that have ever been,

171

A hundred more than men have seen;
She bent the heavens like a bow,
And by that road descended low
Into the land where Morpheus lives:
Strange is that land; its frontier gives
Upon Chimaeria – so tells
The poet. And the house where dwells
That God of Sleep, is stranger still.

2990 There is a cave beneath a hill,
Where no sun shines, nor any light
Brings difference between day and night.
There is no fire, there is no spark;
There is no door which, in that dark,
Might creak to waken sleepers: all
That lies within that slumbrous hall
Is dim and silent; all things keep,
Unhindered, the soft laws of sleep.
Nor, in the country round about

3000 Do broad trees put their branches out
For noisy crow or chattering pie
To perch on them and caw or cry.
There is no cock to crow up day,
Nor any animal that may
Disturb the hill; but all around
Lie, thickly growing on the ground,
Poppies, the wombs of sleepy seeds,
And other drowsy herbs and weeds.
And underneath that hill there flows

3010 A gently moving stream, which goes
Quietly over tiny stones:
This River Lethe's murmured tones
Give listeners great appetite
For sleep. And full of such delight
The House of Sleep is. Of his bed
Within, a little must be said:
Its timbers you would find to be

Of ebony,* that sleepy tree;
The better that he may sleep soft,
On feather beds piled high aloft   3020
He lies, with many a pillow of down;
And, all about the chamber strown,
Dreams multiply a thousandfold. . . .

[*To Morpheus, in these surroundings, Iris comes with her
message, and bids him transmit it to Halcyone. She thereupon
dreams that Ceyx is lying naked and drowned upon the sea-
shore. In the morning, she investigates, and the dream proves
true. Pitying her grief, the Gods restore Ceyx to life, and turn
the couple into Kingfishers. Dreams may therefore, says the
Confessor, be veridical; but this is no excuse for somnolence.
Gower again denies having slept when duty bade him wake. The
Confessor is pleased, and proceeds to tell a story of how love
and sleep accord ill together. It is for the most part original,
though suggested by Ovid.*]

CONFESSOR:

If any man for love would wake
By night, let him example take
From Cephalus when he was laid
Beside Aurora, that fair maid,   3190
Between her arms the whole long night.
But when it drew towards the light,
And he within his heart saw clear
The day's dawning drawing near,
Then for delight of love he prayed
Unto the Sun; and thus he said:
'Phoebus, who governest the light
Of day, until that it be night;
Who cheerest everything that lives

* Ovid has, in the ablative, *ebeno*, which is clearly 'ebony' – the
wood having been chosen for its colour. Gower is confusing this
with some earlier version of Shakespeare's 'cursed Hebanon' – a
poisonous soporific.

3200 (For this is law thy nature gives) –
There is one matter, none the less,
Which only to the consciousness
Belongs in utter privacy'
To love and all his equity:
Which asketh not to be revealed,
But all in silence, and concealed,
Desireth to be overshaded.
And thus, then, when thy light has faded,
And Vesper shows himself aloft,
3210 And when the nights are long and soft,
Under the cloudbanks dark and still,
Then most this matter hath its will.
Therefore, oh Potency most high,
Because thou art the morning's eye,
And showest all, in love's despite:
In this dark season of the night
To thee, with all my heart, I pray
That I may seek my joy, and stay,
With her who lieth in my arms.
3220 Withdraw the banner of thine Arms,
And let thy splendours be unborn;
And in the Sign of Capricorn,*
The House where Saturn dwells, I pray
That thou wilt both abide and stay,
Where nights are dark and long. For see,
My love is gathered unto me
And lies here naked by my side,
As one who would be open-eyed;
Nor have I wish, nor have I need,
3230 For sleep: 'twere good if thou tookst heed
Of this my plight and this my prayer,
And shouldst be pleased to guide through air

* The sun enters the sign of Capricorn on 21 December. There-
fore, since the metal of Saturn is Lead, and the season is midwinter,
a heavy slowness of pace is presumed. See Book Seven, l.
1169 f.

Thy fiery Chariot so ordained
That thy swift horses be restrained
Low under Earth, in the Occident:
So should they to the Orient
Go round the rim the longer way.
Thou too, Diana: thee I pray –
For thy nobility and might
Called Moon and Goddess of the Night,   3240
That thou be gracious to me, and
In thine own House,* the Crab, shalt stand
Opposed to Phoebus all this while,
Gazing on Venus with the smile
Of thy delight and of thy brow:
In such a starry pattern thou
Art patroness of increase – thus
Astrology instructeth us –
And quickenest the womb. If we,
Lady, might have such grace of thee,   3250
With all my heart then would I serve
By night, thy vigil to observe.'

[*Genius draws the obvious moral once more. Gower replies to him.*]

GOWER:

Father, a man who has his love
All naked, lying by his side,
If he could then be heavy-eyed
With sleep, what kind of man is he?
I must assure you, as for me,   3280
I never knew it happen yet.
But now and then, if I did get
A snatch of sleep because I lay
Alone, and if my dreams were gay
Before the passing of the night;

---

* i.e. Zodiacal sign. Since Gower's rhetorical intention is obvious, there is small point in explaining, here, the astrological references involved. See Book Seven, l. 978 f.

And if it happened that I might
Dream of such phantasies as pleased,
I felt I was a little eased –
For other comforts have I none.
3290 I have no need to pray the Sun
Hold back his Chariot, and tarry;
Nor yet Diana, that she carry
Her course through heaven a few hours more:
I am no better paid therefor
With Love, in any least degree.

[*The Confessor agrees, but tells one more story to prove the
dangers of Somnolence. It is the tale of how Mercury piped
Argus to sleep in order to steal Io; it comes from Book One of
the* Metamorphoses. *And so to the last kind of Sloth, which
is* Tristesse *or Despondency. This vice has a companion,
Obstinacy, who keeps* Tristesse *from listening to reason. Where
one is, the other will be found. Gower confesses to guilt in
respect of despair in love; and, as a warning, is told the story of
Anaxarete* (Metamorphoses, Book Fourteen – *though Gower
has made some alterations). Iphis, son of King Teucer, loved
Anaxarete, a girl of lowly birth. She, however, would have
nothing to do with him.*]

CONFESSOR:

While this mad love pervades his soul,
3530 Cold reason holds her in control;
And she, for dread of shame, eschews
The pleasures that his heart pursues;
And, as is right, she held in dread
The losing of her maidenhead.
The matter wavered in debate
Between his lust and her estate:
By gifts, by letter, and by word,
He wooed till, hope so long deferred
For all that he could do or say,
3540 At length he cast that hope away

And gave his heart up to despair.
Daily he pined in grief and care,
Till he had withered from delight,
Desire, and sleep, and appetite. ...

[*On a dark, moonless night he comes to Anaxarete's gate and after a long and formal complaint, hangs himself from the doorpost. In the morning, Anaxarete is filled with passionate remorse.*]

CONFESSOR:

And thus, full piteously, said she:
'Ah God, thou knowst it was for me
That Iphis suffered so today:
So rule the world that men shall say,
A thousand winters after this,
That I, a maiden, did amiss.
And as I did, so do to me;
For, as I showed no charity
To him, to my lost love, from you
I must expect no pity, too.'   3630
She swooned away upon the word,
And lay there low, and never stirred.
The Gods had heard the girl complain,
Saw her repentance and her pain,
And, from the living flesh and bone,
They changed her into lifeless stone –
A statue both in form and face
Like to the maiden in her grace.
Hearing the wonder of this thing,
Thither the Queen came, and the King,   3640
And many of the courtiers too;
And when they saw that it was true
And that, as you have heard above,
Iphis had killed himself for love
Which Anaxarete refused,
Of guilt they held all men excused –
But wondered at her penalty.

177

So, to preserve her memory,
They took that lovely stony thing,
3650   In cortège rich and glittering,
With torches, pomp, and artifice,
Back to the town of Salamis.
And thither too the youth for whom
She died, they bore; there in one tomb,
By royal order, should be laid
The dead prince and the statue-maid.

[*But the statue is set upon a high pillar in the temple of
Venus, and the prince buried beneath it in a tomb of jasper
and marble. Before passing on to the next of the seven sins, we
are given Iphis's epitaph, which runs as follows:*
3674   *Here Iphis lies, a youth self-slain*
For love of Anaxarete.
Here stands her image: let it be
A sign to women, lest again
Their coldness cause the deaths of men,
And they, like it, from flesh and bone,
3680   *Be frozen in a form of stone.*
He was too tender, she too hard:
Take heed, you who come afterward. . . .]

Book Five: Avarice

CONFESSOR:

WHEN first Almighty God began
This world, before the race of Man
Was numbered in its multitudes,
There was no strife for worldly goods:
All things were held in common; men
Took never a thought for riches then,
Nor spoke of profit or of loss –
Till Avarice drew his trail across
A world grown full of men and flocks,
And many a horse and many an ox,   10
Where money made its own increase.
Out of the window then went peace,
And in came war on every side;
Love, thrust into a corner, died;
And common wealth was private made:
So that, instead of shovel and spade,
The biting sword was taken out.
And in this way it came about
That all men made their ditches deep,
And built their walls up high, to keep   20
That gold which Avarice encloses
(And is too scant, as he supposes,
Though the world's wealth were not so much).
For all that comes within his clutch,
In money, or in goods or land,
Shall never slip from out his hand:
He will have more, and hold it fast,
As if this world were built to last.
And therein he resembles Hell;
For, as the ancient writings tell,   30
What enters there – both great and small –

Shall nevermore depart at all;
So, having locked his money-box,
He nevermore undoes the locks –
Unless he longs to have a sight
Of all his gold, so fair and bright,
And brood and gloat on it awhile;
He dares adopt no other style
Of use, or spending. So, be sure,
40 Though he has plenty, he is poor;
And, in the midst of wealth, he lacks.
The sheep have wool upon their backs,
But own it not: there comes a day
When shearers take their fleece away;
An ox that pulls a plough, again,
Earns little profit from his pain;
A miser has, and yet has not,
Who never uses wealth, once got.
And so, for people of discretion,
50 To call such wealth as his 'possession',
Is to be very imprecise:
His wealth owns *him*; as in a vice
It holds him prisoner, a thrall
Who has no real delight at all;
Who should be master of his pelf,
But finds he is a slave himself.
All money-misers are made thus.
My son, since thou art amorous,
Hast thou in loving acted so?

GOWER:

60 My father – to my knowledge – no.
I have not had a chance to be,
As you present the case to me
And as you set it out, above:
In full possession of my love
I never have been, to this day;
Thus, it appears to me, I may

Acquit myself of avarice.
I dare, however, own to this:
If I obtained that treasure, I
Should watch it with a jealous eye,   70
And hold it to my bosom fast,
Until the God of Love at last
Caused death to make me let it go.
For, be assured, I love her so,
That were she my sweet lusty wife,
Then I would guard her with my life;
Were she compliant to my will,
Forever would I guard her still:
Thus would I hoard her, be it known,
If once I had her for my own;   80
Yet though I hoarded this repast,
Not once a-Fridays would I fast.
Fie on the purses in the chest!
Might I but kiss her, I were blest.
Assuredly, if she were mine,
To me that were a dearer *mine*
Than gold: the wealth of all the earth
Could never make me of such worth
As then. She has such wealth within,
I count all else not worth a pin;   90
Were I possessed of such a thing,
Then had I treasure for a King;
To hold it fast, as then I would,
Were only doing as I should.
But now I must forgo the same,
And whistle after smaller game –
Though with bad grace, for thus I would
Be avaricious if I could.

[*The Confessor understands, but cannot wholly approve,
Gower's attitude. He tells the story of Midas – based upon
Book Eleven of the* Metamorphoses. *Silenus was the priest of
Bacchus, God of Wine. One night in Phrygia he was drunk and*

*incapable, and was brought in bonds before Midas, the King
of that country. Midas recognized him, and treated him
courteously. In gratitude, Bacchus offered the King any worldly
thing he might choose. Midas debated within himself.*]

[MIDAS:]

Mankind has but three kinds of treasure:
Wealth, honoured power, and merest pleasure.
Now, if I were to crave that third,
190   And should obtain it on the word,
Still I should lose it, growing old;
Fickle it is, and not to hold,
And fleshly joys all end in woe:
I will not ask for pleasure. No,
But if I ask dominion
Of all the world, and worship won,
Then I have but an occupation
For my puffed-up imagination –
My heart within me will be vain,
200   But I have none the surer gain;
Who can tell emperor from slave,
Before the crib or past the grave?
And if I ask for profit, well,
There is no way that I can tell
To keep my worldly wealth secure:
For riches are the robber's lure,
And wealth attracts the waiting thief;
Such profit only brings men grief. . . .

[*And so on. At length he thinks of gold, and of all that it can
do.*]

CONFESSOR:

Thus in his heart he sang the praise
Of gold.
        [MIDAS:]
        In value it outweighs
All other metals; is prized most;

Gold may call out a mighty host
To carry war against a king;
Gold bears the bell in everything,
And sets the humblest man aloft;
Gold strengthens love, turns hatred soft,
Makes war from peace, and right from wrong;
Turns long to short and short to long;　　240
Where gold is not, there is no feast;
Gold is the lord of man and beast,
Able to have them bought or sold:
Truly, a man might say of gold,
It is what all the world obeys.

CONFESSOR:

To Bacchus, therefore, Midas prays
For gold – but in his prayer exceeds
The measure of his real needs.
Men say that in the malady
Called dropsy, similarity　　250
Exists, with this our present vice
Which we entitle Avarice:
The more the poor hydroptic drinks,
The more he wants to – and he thinks
His thirst impossible to sate;
Thus there is nothing can abate
His longing and his appetite.
Now, it is in this very plight
That Avarice stands and always stood:
The more he has, that he thinks good　　260
To swallow into sightlessness,
The more he wishes to possess.
And just this madness for possession
Laid hold upon the King's discretion;
Avarice clasped him in its clutch –
And all the world might see as much.
For now the Phrygian monarch prayed
That wheresoever his hand were laid,

Whatever he might touch or hold,
270   Should on the instant turn to gold.
This the God Bacchus granted: how
Delighted was King Midas now!
And so he makes all speed he may
To put his power to assay:
He touches that – he touches this –
And in his hands true gold it is,
Pebble and tree and leaf and flower
And fruit and grass, upon the hour.
He went on touching, till at last
280   He felt an urge to break his fast;
For hunger is a natural need,
And, being weary, he must feed.
The cloth was laid, and everything
Set on the board before the king –
His dish and cup, his wine and meat;
But when he tried to drink or eat,
All, ere the King could sip or chew,
Was turned to gold: and then he knew
The folly of his Avarice.

[*Bacchus forgave him, saying that if he bathed in the River
Pactolus, his power would depart. This is why the river and
its gravel bed are now golden. Midas put away avarice thence-
forth; but he serves as a warning to us: coinage is the root of evil:*

    It was the florin, be it known,
    That mothered all our malison.

*We are now told the familiar story of Tantalus, and once
more warned against Avarice, before the Confessor embarks
upon his next subject. This is Jealousy: men become jealous who
are themselves insufficiently virile. Then jealousy is like a fever
within them, and they spend their lives spying upon their ladies.
If they are married, then both live in misery, and must forgo
the true delights of love – for jealousy is itself a kind of avarice.
By way of illustration, we are given the tale of how Vulcan
found Venus his wife in bed with Mars, bound them together*

*with chains, and would have shamed them before the other gods:
but it was he who was put to shame. Gower, somewhat arti-
ficially, protests that there is only one God. Genius replies that
various gods have been worshipped in various places: the
Chaldees worshipped Sun, Moon, and Stars, and the Elements;
the Egyptians worshipped animals, but also a few anthropo-
morphic deities. The Greeks made gods of great men, but also
had the pantheon of familiar mythology. Venus, moreover, the
daughter of Saturn, and mother of Cupid by her brother Jupiter,
was the first goddess to teach men that love should be common,
and to persuade women to sell themselves.*

*Then came the Hebrews, who flourished until the birth of
Christ, but then declined. Only in Christ's faith can we hope
for salvation; but we are miserable sinners, and not least
among our sins is Avarice: and the next kind of Avarice is
Covetousness. An example of covetousness occurs in the story
of Virgil's Mirror, which appears in the* Roman des Sept
Sages. *The magician Virgil set up a huge mirror, outside
Rome, in which could be seen all enemies for thirty miles
around. The Carthaginians took counsel with the King of
Apulia, how they might destroy this mirror. Now Crassus, the
Roman Emperor, was covetous; so Carthaginian envoys were
able to trick him into believing that a treasure was concealed
beneath the mirror. He undermined the structure; the mirror fell
in ruins, and Hannibal was able to inflict a grievous defeat upon
Rome. The Romans punished Crassus by pouring molten gold
down his throat, so as to quench his thirst for that metal.
Another story follows immediately.]*

CONFESSOR:

A chronicle I read says this:
A certain King, as custom is,
Had knights and squires about his court,
And officers of every sort;
For years this multitude had served,
And some now thought that they deserved
Advancement – but must do without

2280 While others of that courtly rout,
In service since but yesterday,
Obtained promotion straight away.
The seniors even dared to bring
Themselves to grumble at the King,
In private, many a time and oft;
But there is never a word so soft
That it is not revealed at last:
The King was told, and forthwith cast
About, as fitted his good sense,
2290 How to provide them evidence
That in complaining of him they
Did not see where the true fault lay.
So, in pursuance of his plan,
Which he concealed from every man,
He had a pair of coffers made,
Identical in form and shade –
So like in workmanship that none
Could tell *this* from the other one.
To his own room he had them brought,
2300 These chests mysteriously wrought,
Because he had ordained that they
Should for a time be locked away.
Then, secretly and cunningly,
He took his opportunity,
And not a courtier could have guessed:
With his own hands he filled one chest
With finest gold and jewellery
Obtained from out his treasury;
And then he took the other box
2310 And weighted it with broken rocks
And stuffed it full as it would go
With rubbish and with straw. And so,
As early as could be, next day,
He called his men to where he lay,
And bade them set before his bed
A trestle table richly spread;

And on this table there should rest
The one chest and the other chest.
The King well knew the names and sort
Of all the grumblers at his court,   2320
In the bed-chamber and the hall;
So now he sent for one and all,
And what he said to them was this:
'Let no man take his luck amiss;
I know how long you all have served,
And God knows what you have deserved:
But whether yours must be the blame
That your advancement never came,
Or whether it belongs to me,
Is what we are about to see –   2330
To set your evil tongues at rest.
Now, this chest or the other chest,
Which here you see upon the board,
Is yours to choose: but one is stored
With so much wealth that, if by wit
Or by good luck you light on it,
You shall be rich men while you live.
Whichever you prefer, I give;
But take good heed which it shall be,
For one of them, I guarantee,   2340
Holds absolutely nothing which
Can profit you or make you rich.
Confer together, that your choice
Be made with no dissenting voice;
For if I do not now advance
Your state, it is the fault of chance
And of no choice except your own.
So in this place it shall be shown
To all at last, that luck, not I,
Determines how your fortunes lie.'   2350
They all knelt down, and with one voice
Began to thank him for this choice;
Then having risen up, they went

Aside, and into argument,
And reached agreement in the end:
To tell the King what they intend,
And to report their mind aright,
As spokesman they appoint a knight.
This knight kneels down before the King
2360 And says that in this dubious thing
They are agreed that he shall choose,
No matter if they win or lose.
He takes a rod into his hand
And goes to where the coffers stand
And, as the agent of the rest,
He lays his rod upon a chest,
And tells the King that this is what
Their guerdon shall be, rich or not,
And begs that they may have it now.
2370 Bound by his honour and his vow,
The King accorded them the choice
Which they had made by common voice,
And thereon handed them the key;
And, resolute to have them see
What wealth they had, as they supposed,
Bade that the contents be disclosed:
And stones and straw were all their lot;
Thus each of them was paid his scot.
But thereupon the King undid
2380 The other box, and raised the lid,
And there they saw more treasure than
Was in the reckoning of man.
'Lo!' said the King, 'you now may see
That blame does not attach to me;
I stand acquitted of that same,
And you yourselves must bear the blame
For what your fortune has refused.'
Thus the wise monarch was excused,
And all gave up their slandering
2390 And begged for mercy from the King.

[*A similar story follows: two beggars are given the choice of two pasties, one containing a capon and the other a store of florins – with the same result as above, and the same moral drawn.*]

CONFESSOR:

And just as all these people stood,
In utter lack of worldly good,
As thou hast heard me say above,
So, often, do men stand in love:
Thou mayst long covet it, and yet
No mite of profit shalt thou get   2450
Beyond what fate intends for thee;
All else is idle. Yet we see
Plenty indeed of those who go
Around, these days, and covet so:
All women such a man may see –
Yes, even ten or twelve, maybe,
So foolish love is, nowadays –
If they have beauty, they will raise
His heart at once to hold them dear.
He whispers nothings in their ear,   2460
Swears he is deeply amorous –
And thus his heart turns covetous.
He seeks to have more than he may:
Though he should see five score a day,
His folly, his mad enterprise
And covetousness, will arise –
And in each one of them will find
Some quality that takes his mind:
One, because she is white of skin;
One, for the grandeur of her kin;   2470
One, for the roses of her cheek;
One, because she looks mild and meek;
One, because she has eyes of grey;
One, because she can laugh and play;
One, because she is tall and slender;
One, because she is small and tender;

One, because she is pale as dough;
One, for her speech is soft and low;
One, for her nose's prominence;
2480   One, for her virgin innocence;
One, because she can sing and dance:
He always finds some circumstance
To please him; though her one appeal
Be that she has a tiny heel,
That is enough to love her for.
Thus will he love a hundred score,
While they are fresh, whom he desires;
But he will scorn them when he tires.
A blind man is no judge of hue;
2490   All is one darkness, to his view;
That man's desire is blinded thus
Whose loving is but covetous.
It seems the world would not suffice
To satisfy him in his vice;
For, if such fortune might befall,
Could he, he would possess them all,
As common as the market-place:
I do not think he stands in grace.

[*Gower denies that he is thus guilty, or – for Genius raises this point too – that he loves his lady for her riches. He loves her for her grace, goodness, and beauty. She has enough, indeed, of worldly goods; but –*

    By Cupid in his Court above,
    I love my lady for pure love.

This is very well, says his Confessor, but proceeds to tell him the story of the King of Apulia and his Steward's wife. This also is derived from the Roman des Sept Sages. *A certain king was advised by his physicians to take a fair young woman into his bed, and so ordered his Steward to provide one. The Steward had in any case married for lucre and not for love; he kept the hundred pounds, which the King had given him for expenses, and forced his own wife into bed with the King.*

When all was discovered, the Steward was banished, and the
woman eventually married the King. So to the next kinds of
Covetousness, which are False Witness and Perjury. Lovers
often, says Genius, obtain their ends by falsely swearing service
to a woman. But False Witness will at last be discovered, as
is proved by the tale of Achilles and Deidamia which Gower
obtained from Statius. When Achilles, in female disguise, hid
himself among women, his bedfellow was Deidamia, daughter
of King Lycomedes. He secretly got her with child, but was
eventually – by a trick – made publicly to disclose both his sex
and the whole truth of the matter. Perjury is exemplified in
the story of Jason and Medea, which Gower derives mainly from
Benoît. This story is so familiar, and told by him at such
enormous length – almost 1,000 lines – that only a summary
and a few excerpts need be given here.

Jason was the son of Aeson, and nephew of the childless
Pelias, King of Iolcus. For political reasons, Jason was sent
by his uncle to seek the Golden Fleece from the island of Colchis,
where Aeëtes tried to dissuade Jason from the quest; but the
King's lovely daughter Medea fell in love with Jason (as he with
her) and promised to help him if he would marry her. This he
gladly swore to do, and they forthwith anticipated the ceremony.
She now told him that to obtain the Fleece he must tame and yoke
two firebreathing oxen which guarded it upon an island near by,
and slay the sleepless and poisonous dragon which kept it. The
oxen must plough a furrow in which the dragon's teeth must be
sown. Warriors would spring up from them, and slay each
other, and at length the Fleece would be his.]

CONFESSOR:

'All these are perils to be passed,'   3541
Medea said to him. 'One last
Provision there is, ere you go,
And one more thing that you must know:
What remedy you may require
Against the venom and the fire.
But, Jason, it is nearly day;

Let us arise, then, that I may
Deliver to you that which will
3550   Preserve your life and honour still.'
Oh both of them were loth to rise;
But yet, since both of them were wise,
They did forsake their bed at last:
With Jason's clothes around him cast,
The Knight was ready thereupon;
And she, her little shift pulled on,
And her close-clinging mantle too,
Was risen without more ado.
Then she took forth a box, thick sown
3560   With gold and many a precious stone,
And out of it she drew a ring
Bejewelled beyond purchasing:
No peril, while he chose to wear it,
She said, but he might safely dare it;
In ocean floods it could not drown,
And, where it came, all fires burned down;
Its power would daunt the cruellest
Of hearts; no evil could molest
Whether by water or by land,
3570   The man who wore it on his hand.
And furthermore, she told him then,
If he would go unseen by men,
Within his palm the stone held tight
Would charm him out of all men's sight.

[*She gives him further instructions, about what prayers and
rituals to employ, an ointment that should preserve him and
his armour, and a certain glue to stop up the fire of the oxen's
breath. Jason and Medea part, with tears and protestations.
He accomplishes his quest, and begins to sail homeward.*]

CONFESSOR:

Medea sighed and wept full oft,
And on a tower high aloft

She stood alone, in secrecy,
And prayed, and murmured inwardly,
'Oh God, oh well may he be sped,
The Knight that had my maidenhead!'   3740
And still she gazed towards the isle;
But then she saw, within a while,
The gold fleece glittering in the sun,
And said, 'Thank God, now all is won;
Out of the field, my Knight wins clear –
But oh, would God that he were here!'
Had she been winged as is the dove,
She would have flown then to her love,
There in the ship; but she could not.

*[So Jason comes to shore, is greeted with great acclamation,
and is kissed by the King in person.]*

CONFESSOR:

Medea would have kissed him too,
For she was wonderfully fain;
But, blushing, she turned back again: 3790
Custom forbade it, then and there,
And so, for shame, she did not dare.
She took her leave, and Jason went
Into his room: thither she sent
Her maid, to see if he was well –
Who, having seen him, and heard tell
Of his adventures far away,
Was sure that he fared well that day.
And when this message was relayed,
For joy, Medea kissed the maid.   3800
And now the bath is full of heat,
With scented herbs to make it sweet;
Jason unarms, and will prepare
To use the comforts ready there;
Then in the bath he washes him
Clean as a bone, in every limb;

He sups, and so comes out anon
And puts his best apparel on,
And combs his hair. So being clad,
3810   Goes forth refreshed, and merry and glad,
Into the King's great Council Hall. . . .

[There he recounts his adventures, amid much wonderment.
Supper-time comes, and Jason is placed beside Medea. They
secretly spend the rest of the night together; but Jason has
made plans to slip away from Colchis; so, in the morning,
Medea robs her father of his treasure and sails away to Greece
with her lover. Aeson, Jason's father, is glad to see them;
but he is almost senile. So Medea, who is skilled in magic,
prepares to restore his youth.]

CONFESSOR:

So it befell, upon a night
When starlight was the only light,
She vanished at her own sweet will,
3960   And no one knew. The world was still,
And the clocks showed the midnight hour:
With hair about her in a shower,
Bareheaded, and her feet all bare,
Out from the palace did she fare.
Her garments girdled high around,
Silent along the grassy ground
She glided as an adder might:
Thus went Medea forth by night
Until she reached the stream she sought,
3970   And there she stood awhile in thought.
Thrice then she turned herself around,
And three times bowed her to the ground;
And thrice, upon the riverside,
Her loose hair trailing in the tide,
She gasped to feel the bitter pain.
But then she caught her breath again:
First she began to call and cry

194

To every star that rides the sky;
To wind and air, to sea and land,
She prayed, and lifted either hand   3980
To Hecate the Witch, for aid. ...

[*A dragon-chariot appears, and takes her to many strange
lands where she gathers the herbs required for Aeson's re-
juvenation. This takes her several days and nights. She returns,
builds altars to Hecate and to Juventas, goddess of youth,
surrounds them with vervain and many other herbs, and digs two
pits near by.*]

CONFESSOR:

Now, a black wether being slain,
She let the blood run out, and drain,
A little into either pit;
Warm milk was then poured into it,
And honey, and round this device
She now began her sacrifice.   4050
And soon her prayers grew clamorous:
To Pluto, Lord of Tartarus,
And to his queen, Persephone,
And so to all the hierarchy
Of them who rule the magic art –
None was forgotten, for her part –
She prayed, past-mistress in this thing,
That Aeson's Winter turn to Spring.
Old Aeson was brought forward then,
And she dismissed all other men,   4060
Lest peril fall on them; they heard,
And all departed at her word,
Leaving the two of them alone.
Then she began to gasp and moan,
Describing many a magic sign,
With cantrips secret and malign;
Then, after all her spells and charms,
She lifted Aeson in her arms;

195

A slumber bound his every limb:
4070 Down on the herbs she settled him.
The flesh of the black sheep she took
And hewed asunder, like a cook,
And part on either altar laid;
Then, with more magic spells, she prayed
Until a fire from heaven lit
A brightly burning flame in it.
And when Medea saw it burn,
Then she began to writhe and turn
Between the altars, and around:
4080 Never a beast that goes on ground
Seems wilder than Medea there.
About her shoulders hung her hair,
As if her wits were stolen away,
And she transfigured. Now, there lay,
Near by, some chips of cloven trees;
Now and again she gathered these
And thrust them in the blood-pits first,
Then in the altar-fires; they burst
Into fierce torches; then she ran
4090 Three times around that ancient man,
Aeson, where on the ground he slept;
Then with some water she had kept,
She drew a circle round him thrice,
And then with burning sulphur twice.
And many another thing she wrought,
Of which, as now, I shall say naught.
Soon she began to run about,
And many a wondrous noise came out:
For now she crowed as does the cock,
4100 Or whistled like the laverock,
Or cackled like a barnyard hen,
And sometimes used the speech of men;
And, as her jargon grew more strange,
So, ever, would her features change.
She seems no woman, but a fay:

Such powers to her charms obey,
She might be called a deity;
For what she wills, apparently,
She does – or so in books we find;
And that surpasses human-kind.   4110
But who would hear of wonders, let
Him heed what matters followed yet:
How she achieved what she began
Are marvels never heard by man.

It was the night of the new moon;
And what must be must happen soon:
She took a cauldron, and put in
The whole of her strange medicine
Of juice, of water, and of blood;
Over the fire this cauldron stood   4120
Until it boiled and on the broth
She saw the rising of white froth;
And then she cast in root and rind
And seed and flower, and many a kind
Of magic herb and mineral
(For this she had compiled them all);
That serpent called Cinyphius*
Lent all his scales to aid her thus;
Chelydrus† gave his aspish skin:
And, all to boil, she cast them in –   4130
With part of that which men hear howl
By night, and fear, the hornéd owl;
And of a raven which men hold
Had been nine hundred winters old,
She took the head and all the beak;
And, lest her medicine be weak,

* There is no such creature. A grammatical misunderstanding
led Gower to believe that the adjective derived from the River
Cinyps (in Libya) was the name of a serpent.
† The Chelydrus – which is mentioned by Virgil – is an un-
certainly identified water-snake.

A sea-wolf's* bowels joined the brew,
That Aeson might be made anew;
She added then a thousand more,
4140 Of things that she had kept in store,
Into the cauldron quickly. Now
She takes a withered olive bough
To stir around the magic brew:
At once it flowers and fruits anew,
And suddenly grows fresh and green.

[*Now Medea knows that her medicine is effective. She drains
off Aeson's blood, and fills his body with her magic broth; he
then drinks some of it, and becomes a lusty young man of twenty.
All is gaiety for a while. Jason, however, soon abandons Medea
and marries the lovely Creusa. Medea sends her a mantle
of cloth-of-gold, magically treated. When Creusa puts it on,
her flesh and bones are burnt up. Now Medea brings their
children to Jason, slays them before his eyes, and is caught up to
Heaven by Minerva – leaving her faithless lover desolate. This
is what comes of swearing false oaths.*

*There follows now the story of Phrixus and Helle. These
were the children of Athamas by his first wife. His second wife,
Ino, intrigued to have them killed; but Juno provided a ram with
a golden fleece, to carry them overseas. Helle fell off and was
drowned, but Phrixus came safely to Colchis. This was the
origin of the Golden Fleece, and of Jason's false oath. Now the
Confessor turns to consider Usury.*]

CONFESSOR:

Who, if he gives or lends to men,
Will ask good measure back again –
He gives a pea to get a bean.
4410 Lovers are many to be seen,
Of this kind: though their love be slight,
So that it scarcely weighs a mite,

---

* 'Sea-wolf' is Gower's phrase, and too good to abandon; but
it means 'shark'.

Lest their usurious bargain lack,
A pound of loving they ask back.

[*Gower denies being usurious in love: indeed, he has always given
far more than he receives. Nor has he ever employed love-
brokers to purchase his lady's love.*]

GOWER:

I have heard tell that thought is free;
So, father, between you and me –
Since you are here at your discretion
To hear the whole of my confession –
My secret heart shall be disclosed.
By usury, I have supposed   4490
That usury in love is meant:
My lady is not innocent!
Yet for one glance of her dear eye,
My inmost heart until I die,
With all that I may do, or can,
Are given her; I am her man.
And does not justice then accord,
From her to me, some small reward,
A little fragment of her all?
God knows what future may befall;   4500
I know that present facts are stern:
No kindly word will she return
To me, in any form or guise,
Whereby my fallen hopes might rise,
And my great love receive its guerdon.
How can her conscience bear the burden
Of all this usury? In great
Abundance, and by ample weight,
She has my love; but I have naught
Of all that I have dearly bought   4510
And paid for with my very heart.
No, no; all that is set apart,
And loveless must I go about.

Ought she not stand in fear and doubt
Until she has redressed that sin,
When all my love is hers to win,
And I have naught by which to live?
She does not even choose to give
A 'thank you', out of which I might
4520 Wring comfort in my pain's despite.
In this I am, in my own eyes,
Like one who pays for merchandise,
And dearly, but receives it not,
And loses all that he has got:
I get no love, who buy it dear;
And I have never yet come near
To winning profit from my love.

Therefore, as I have said above,
Of usury I am clear-quit;
4530 And if my lady practise it,
I pray to God that he may send
Grace that shall cause her to amend.

CONFESSOR:

My son, your answer – every word –
Concerning usury, is heard.
Albeit thy reward is small,
In love, I do not think that all
Thy plaint is just: words are misused
If thine own lady stands accused.
Thou hast already said that by
4540 A single glance of her dear eye
Thy heart was her inheritance:
It may be that her single glance
Is worth thy heart – yea, manifold;
And so thy heart is dearly sold,
For thou hast more than thou art given.
And, be her weight of love uneven
With thine, as thou hast further said,

Two equal loves were never wed
By Heaven on those tilting scales
Wherein Love's governance prevails.   4550
It is a statute of Love's law
That though thy mistress overdraw
Against thy love, or thine weigh more,
Thou mayst ask no return therefor
Of right, but as an act of grace.
Since Love is lord in every place,
No law, however mild or grim,
Has any power over him;
But he will act as he may choose,
To make men either win or lose.   4560

Lovers are light when they begin;
But whether they shall lose or win,
That is what every man learns last:
My son, go not about too fast
To covet, but abide thine end;
Who knows but all thy grief shall mend?

[*At least, says the Confessor, he is sure that Gower has not committed brokerage in love – whereof an awful warning is the case of the nymph Echo. This tale comes from Ovid's Metamorphoses, Book Three. Echo used to deceive her mistress, Juno, by procuring new bedfellows for Jupiter. She was punished for this by being condemned to dwell among woods and hills, and – she who had not spoken when she should – only to repeat the voices of others. This is an example not merely to unfaithful husbands, but to love-brokers.*

The next follower of Avarice is Parsimony or Meanness:

> *Who takes, and keeps, and holds, and stints,*
> *Till it were easier flaying flints*
> *Than getting him, by foul or fair,*
> *To yield the value of a tare.*

Gower denies all guilt in this respect.]

GOWER:

My father, it stands thus with me:
4730   If Croesus' entire treasury,
With Emperor Octavian's gold,
And Indian riches manifold,
Of pearls and every precious stone,
Should all at once become my own,
Yet I would rate the whole of this
No higher than a straw's worth is;
The self-same day it should be laid
In gift before that sweetest maid,
That she might scorn me one jot less.
4740   It is no sin of thriftiness,
Good father, you may well believe,
That makes me hopeless to achieve
The purpose which is all my thought.
And yet, I never gave her ought,
Nor ever dared so much as proffer:
I know she would refuse my offer,
For she will neither take nor give –
To both alike, pure negative –
Because, unless I reason ill,
4750   In my case it is not her will
To give me cause for hoping, not
The very smallest crumb or jot.
With other folk, as well I see,
She takes and gives so lavishly
(Within the bounds of friendship and
Of chastity, you understand),
That all men praise her not a little.
Of me, she will not take a tittle,
Though well aware that if I could
4760   Bear her both love and gifts, I would,
And strive to please with all my might.
This, all men know, who think aright,
And from this law they cannot part:

She who is mistress of one's heart,
Is mistress of one's worldly goods.

[*Well said, replies the Confessor, for love and parsimony go ill together,*

*And many a time a man has lost
His coat, because he skimped the hood.*

Now follows the story of Babio and Croceus. Babio was in love with Viola, but was niggardly. When she met Croceus, who was both lusty and liberal, it was the latter who obtained her favours. So to the next vice, which is Ingratitude. This is illustrated by the tale of Adrian and Bardus. Adrian, a great Roman lord, was hunting and by chance fell into a pit. There he lay all day calling for help, until towards evening a poor man called Bardus passed by, leading a donkey loaded with wood. Adrian heard him, and promised him half his own wealth in return for help. Bardus let down a rope, and was amazed when it drew up not Adrian but an ape which had also fallen in. The rope went down a second time, and drew up a serpent. Only at the third attempt did Adrian rise to the surface – and, without a word of thanks, made his way homeward. Poor Bardus took it philosophically, and went out again, next day, to gather more wood.]

CONFESSOR:

When he drew near his usual place,   5051
There stood the ape before his face;
It had been gathering, all this while,
Of wood and sticks a goodly pile,
All ready laid to Bardus' hand.
He trussed and bound his bundles; and
The ape continued, day by day,
To help its saviour in this way,
So that he never lacked for wood.
One day, soon after, Bardus stood   5060
Beside the forest; there he spied
The huge and ghastly serpent glide
Towards him; and, when it reached him quite,

All such obeisance as it might
It did him. And then, last of all,
Out of its mouth the snake let fall
A stone more bright than crystal is;
It went its way then, Bardus his.

[*This jewel was sold for a vast sum of money; yet, on returning home, Bardus found that it was back in his purse. This happened every time he sold the stone, so that he quickly grew rich. The Emperor heard about him, was told the whole story, and punished the lord Adrian. Beware of ingratitude! Gower says that not he, but his lady, is ungrateful. Genius reproves him, and tells him a further story – that of how Ariadne helped Theseus to slay the Minotaur, and was then seduced and abandoned by him. Thus he broke the laws of love, and was afterwards punished for it.*

Next, the Confessor turns to Rapine, the forcible seizure of other men's goods. Gower is shocked to hear of lovers who behave so; but he must listen to the story of Tereus, Procne, and Philomela. The Confessor tells this story well, but at excessive length. It is in any case familiar, and may be found in Metamorphoses, *Book Six – and elsewhere. King Tereus raped and mutilated Philomela, who was horribly avenged by her sister Procne. In the end, Tereus was turned into a lapwing, the falsest of birds; Procne into a swallow, for ever twittering warnings; Philomela into a nightingale, for ever lamenting her stolen virginity. 'My son,' says Genius, 'never act like Tereus of Thrace.' 'God forbid,' says Gower, 'I would rather be torn to pieces by wild horses, than do the smallest thing against Love's laws and my lady's will.' Another aspect of Rapine is Robbery.*]

CONFESSOR:

As thieves will seek what they may win
By robbery, all round about
In woods and fields, where men go out,
So among lovers there are some
6110   Who, in wild places, if they come

Upon a woman apt for it –
And if the time and place be fit –
Will ask no leave, but, ere they rise,
Will meddle with her merchandise.
Yea, though she were a shepherdess,
Yet will this Lord of Wantonness
Attempt her, though she be not meet;
For stolen fruits, they say, are sweet.
At home, unknowing, sits his wife,
Who loves her husband more than life,   6120
And wishes for no better thing
Than his awaited homecoming.
And when her lord returns at eve,
Then he will make his wife believe
Only what *he* declares is true:
He tells her how the huntsmen blew,
How splendidly the hounds have run,
And of the brightness of the sun,
And how his falcons flew the best.
But every word will be suppressed,   6130
Of his betraying Love that day;
How like a robber on the way,
He slaked his lust within the shade –
Whereby Love's laws were disobeyed.

And therefore I forbid, my son,
That such an ill deed should be done.

[*There follows the story of Neptune and the nymph* Cornix,
which is drawn from Metamorphoses, *Book Two. Cornix, a
lovely handmaiden of Pallas, was disporting herself one day on
the beach when Neptune looked on her with lust.*]

CONFESSOR:

Then he resolved with in his heart
That she in nowise should depart,   6170
Without a price, from where they were;

But he himself would pillage her –
Not of her brooches or her rings;
They were quite other little things
He would enjoy before she went.
He clasped her then, incontinent,
And groped towards that treasure-chest
Whose contents he would fain molest –
To steal that jewel which is far
6180   More dear than other treasures are,
And which is called Virginity,
The flower of all things womanly.
This maiden Cornix, all aflame
With terror and with utter shame,
Saw it was vain to vie or plead;
His lust would certainly succeed,
His violence force her to comply.
Then she began to weep and cry,
With, 'Pallas, oh my noble queen,
6190   Now let thy potency be seen,
To keep my honour safe, this day;
Nor let my rose be thieved away,
Which now is sealed beneath thy care!'
This word still hung upon the air,
When Pallas did as she was prayed,
And answered the imploring maid
With full and clear deliverance;
For in this woeful circumstance,
The nymph was changed, upon the word,
6200   From a fair maiden to a bird.
And thus the books recount that he,
The lustful monarch of the sea,
Failed of his robberish attack.
With feathers of a coaly black,
Out of his arms, like bolt from bow,
She flew in likeness of a crow:
And this, to her, was more delight –
To keep her maiden treasure white

Beneath a feather cloak of black –
Than, pearly-skinned, to lose and lack   6210
What never can return again.

[*Another, and better-known, story follows: that of the princess
Callisto. This is also, basically, from Book Two of the* Meta-
morphoses. *Callisto desired to live a virgin among the nymphs
of Diana. Jupiter, however, seduced her and got her with child.
Her secret was discovered when, one day, she was forced to bathe
naked with her mistress and the nymphs. Having borne a son,
Arcas, she was transformed by Diana into a bear.*

*Now comes a long passage in praise of virginity. Not only
is it lovely in itself, says Genius, but evil follows when it is
forcibly ravished. Gower understandably objects that general
virginity would depopulate the world; his Confessor answers that
virginity must be surrendered only according to Love's laws, and,
in any case, never stolen. Next we pass to Stealthy Thievishness
or* Mecherie.]

CONFESSOR:

Of whom I say, for truth it is,
The peacock's prowling strut is his –
To seize his prey so covertly
That none see through that secrecy.   6500
When husbands have been called from home,
He spies his time to stalk and roam;
For, when he knows the men are gone,
Whatever he may come upon
He steals, and passes on his way –
And, who the thief was, none can say.
Or many a time he goes by night,
No moon or star to give him light,
By art unpicks a bolted door,
And takes his pleasure of men's store.   6510
Or, if the door is locked so fast
That even he may not get past,
In at the window he will creep;
And, since the lord is fast asleep,

Again he plunders at his will
And slips away unnoticed still.
Full often, too, by light of day,
He gives his thievish efforts play;
Under your cloak his fingers flit,
6520 And suddenly your purse is slit
And all that it contained is gone.
So thus his gambols will go on
While, what his plans are, no man knows:
He bears a horn he never blows,
And all he earns from pilfering
Is – as one says – beak under wing.
And as a hound, that went to kill
Among the sheep, and take its fill,
Will wipe its bloody jaws on grass
6530 And, in feigned virtue, slink and pass –
And, be his havoc huge and grim,
No shepherd thinks of blaming him,
Nor ever finds the murderer: so,
If he seeks plunder, Stealth will go
Unchallenged in whatever place.
He can so well present his case,
And flatter and pretend so well,
No one on earth could ever tell
His cunning from pure innocence;
6540 And thus he blinds them with pretence.

All this applies directly to
Another sort of crafty crew:
For lovers may act stealthily,
Enjoy their pleasures privily,
Attain to their desires by stealth –
And often find themselves in wealth,
While they may have the use of it.
Such lovers wait, and bend their wit,
To follow up and catch their prey;
6550 And, sure enough, they find a way;

For whether it were day or night,
They would steal something, if they might:
And, if there were no more to do,
Still they would steal a kiss or two.
Tell on, my son, and say if thou
Hast ever acted so, ere now.

GOWER:

In what way, father?

CONFESSOR:

        Son, like this:
If thou didst ever steal a kiss,
Or other dainty from her platter,
Such thefts are not a hanging matter: 6560
Open thy heart, and tell me so.

GOWER:

More is the pity, father, no.
My heart is thievish, though, I fear;
Yet she who is to me most dear,
Being alone and safe with me,
I dare not even clasp her knee,
Or steal from her the smallest bit –
Or she would let me know of it!

[*Nevertheless, he says, he has imagined such thefts, and would
dearly like to commit them:*

    But, by the snake which never slept,
    The golden fleece was never kept
    (In Colchis, as the tale is told)
    So well as, many thousandfold,
    My love is watched and warded in.
    Clad in her clothes or in her skin,
    She has a guardian night and day
    To keep her body from assay.

As may be guessed, this guardian is our old friend Danger (see note on Book One, l. 2443), who permits Gower no liberties at all. As for entering houses stealthily by night, Gower has often stood night long gazing at his lady's window, longing for some means of entry. Genius disapproves, and tells him the story of Leucothoë (Metamorphoses, Book Four, though Gower has modified the tale). The god Phoebus loved the beautiful virgin Leucothoë, who was kept shut up by her mother. So, one day, he crept in through the wall of her room, and stole what he desired. All was discovered, and the girl was buried alive. Phoebus, however, transformed her into a sunflower. Next comes the story of Hercules and Faunus. Hercules and his love Iolë rested together in a cave. Faunus, desiring her, came by night to enjoy her by stealth; but in the darkness he found the wrong pallet, made his attempt upon Hercules instead, and was badly injured. After summing up, the Confessor now turns to Sacrilege, and specifically the sacrilege of lovers.]

CONFESSOR:

Unless to pass an idle time,
They never heed the church-bells' chime,
Not though they see the priest at Mass:
These they ignore, and let them pass.
And should, in church, their love appear,
7040   They stand and whisper in her ear:
Even within that holy place
They ask of God no other grace;
But ere they go they will obtain
Some little token, some small gain –
A promise or a loving word –
Or at the least will see conferred
Some ring or glove her hand makes dear:
Thus closely to the wind they steer,
And say, 'These tokens I have got
7050   Are signs you will forget me not.'
And thus they hallow the High Mass.
Such theft the Church must needs let pass;

They will obey their own sweet will
No matter who may take it ill.

In the great cities we shall find
More people of the selfsame kind –
Given to pleasure, blithe and gay –
Who wait upon the holiday
And then, in church and minster, go
To see the womenfolk on show.   7060
This kind of man will strut about
Before the fairest of the rout
Where they are sitting all a-row;
There he will let his body show,
Set on his well-combed crocquet-curl*
A chaplet, or a brooch of pearl,
Or else a leafy coronal
New gathered from the grove – and all
To make himself look trim and fresh.
And then he gazes on their flesh   7070
Like any falcon at the sight
Of prey on which to stoop and light;
As if he came from fairyland,
Thus will he pose before them, and
Profane that holy place: all that,
To make their hearts go pit-a-pat.
His roving eye is never still,
But flits and stares and takes its fill
Of her, and her, with glad surmise;
And every now and then he sighs: 7080
Thinks one of them, 'That was for me' –
Which thought occurs to two or three;
And yet he loves them not at all,
Except as fortune may befall.

[Gower denies having committed any such sacrilege, except that

* This was an elaborate roll of intertwined hair which in
Gower's day was considered a very dashing coiffure indeed.

*even in church he cannot keep his eyes off his lady. And, now
and again – even in church – he sometimes puts his arm around
her waist: he has no pious thoughts when she is near. The
Confessor reproves him, and tells – at considerable length –
the familiar story of Paris and Helen, his moral being that the
fall of Troy was a punishment for Paris's sacrilege in stealing
Helen from the temple of Venus.*

*Avarice, he continues, has a contrary vice, which is Prodigality
– and between them stands Largesse, or Generosity, which is a
virtue. Prodigality is a vice of thoughtlessness.]*

CONFESSOR:

7663 He gives and squanders here and there,
Both careless and forgetful where.
While he may borrow, he will spend;
And though he tries, towards the end,
To call a halt, he is too late:
For poverty is at his gate
And plucking at his very sleeve ...

[*And so on, to further praise of Largesse. But even Largesse
may be overdone.*]

CONFESSOR:

While yet a man has aught to give,
Gay is the life that he may live,
With friends and parties everywhere;
7750 All men's report of him is fair.
While there are bulges in his pack,
'Jack's a fine fellow, who but Jack?'
But when the well runs dry at last,
Their praise is somewhat overcast;
They sing another lyric then –
'Old Jack? He was the best of men.'
And when they see him pass them by,
Needy and poor, it's 'Jack, good-bye.'

[Some folk are thus prodigal of their love, which they fritter away in half a dozen places at once. This is a sin — which Gower denies having committed.]

CONFESSOR:

Son, what thou tellst me may well be.　　　7810
Nevertheless, it is my thought
That all the evil thou hast wrought,
The hours which thou hast let run waste,
May all, by mercy, be replaced.
Perhaps, if things are worth the cost,
They are not wasted, are not lost;
Of what is all uncertainty,
No earthly creature, verily,
Can say what future may portend,
But waits to see how it will end:　　　7820
And so, my son, I cannot say
As yet, if thou art cast away.
What man is there who has not seen
The end of summer and its green,
And winter standing waste and bare
And all the world forlorn and spare?
But the cold wind shall blow its fill,
The sharply driving rain grow still;
And, as it were upon the hour,
Men shall behold the sudden flower,　　　7830
And summer meeting it with glory.
Such, I believe, shall be thy story:
Poor as thou art in grace, my son,
The love thou lack'st may yet be won.

[A formal tail-piece brings the book to its end.]

Book Six: Gluttony

CONFESSOR:

SIN's great and awful origin,
By which all we are born to sin,
The sin that poisons all on Earth,
In Eden had its hideous birth:
First, Adam found the apple sweet,
But then he felt the morsel's heat,
For death descended on mankind.
Read ancient books, and thou shalt find
This vice, that has so utterly
Corrupted us, is Gluttony –
A tree that has so many boughs
That neither time nor space allows
My touching upon more than two;
And that is what I mean to do.
Drunkenness, first, is as it were
The boon companion's cupbearer.
What wonders bear this vice's rule!
It turns a wise man to a fool,
And makes a fool believe his mind
Holds lore and law of every kind –
The workings of the universe
Are easy for him to rehearse;
He understands both stars and moon.
So Drunkenness can very soon
Make scholar out of idiot:
Nothing at all – so thinks the sot –
Too hard for him to understand.
He knows the sea, he knows the strand,
He is a splendid warrior (though
His arms may be as soft as dough);
Strong though he may have been before,

214

When drunken he is strong no more:
How changed is his condition then,
Feeblest and sorriest of men!
For he can neither walk nor run,
And all his powers are undone;
His hands and feet obey him not,
He must stay rooted to the spot.
Then, all his wits have gone astray –
Which hinders him in such a way,   40
He knows not what he is about;
Falsehood and truth must rest in doubt;
He cannot tell high noon from night,
Can recognize no man aright,
And does not know so much as this:
What kind of animal he is,
Nor whether he is man or beast.
Now, this I call a sorry feast,
When all such reason as he had
Is lost; so quickly to grow mad –   50
Or else to be hauled off to bed
As numb and speechless as the dead,
And lie there nightlong, unaware
Of who or how or why or where,
Until he rises on the morrow:
And then he says, 'Ah me! What sorrow
It is, to be a thirsty man!'
Half-drunk, as quickly as he can,
With a dry mouth, he staggers up
And calls, 'Hey! Pour me out a cup!'   60

[*And so forth. But, says the Confessor, never was a man so besotted with drink as even the wisest of men have been with love. Gower acknowledges his guilt in this respect:*

> *Ah, holy father, all is true*
> *That you recount; and I admit*
> *That I am quite undone by it –*
> *My heart is so completely sunk*

215

In Love, that I am reeling drunk.
Although I have both speech and motion,
Yet many a time I have no notion
Of what I do or what I mean.

When he is absent from his lady, he is drunk with thinking of
her; in her presence, he is drunk with the sight of her. The more
he drinks, the more he thirsts: his only cure would be a taste of
the drink that he truly desires, but that he is forbidden to have.
Love-drunkenness, the Confessor admits, although a grievous
thing, is irresistible. Jupiter has in his cellar two tuns of (love)
wine, one sweet and the other bitter. Cupid serves men from
both of these; and, being blind, confuses them. Gower's only
hope is prayer: when Bacchus was dying of thirst in the Lybian
desert, he prayed to Jupiter; a wether appeared, and struck the
ground with its foot; forthwith, a spring of clear water gushed
out. Pray, then; because –

Few men give acres to the dumb:
Think of that proverb, and become
Wise in the virtue of its words.

In the meantime, consider what may happen to those who are
drunk with love – and the story of Tristram and Iseult is told.
Two more tales follow.]

CONFESSOR:

I find accounts in poesy*
Of that most fair Hippodamë,
Of whose great beauty there was word
In all men's mouths. Now, it occurred
That young Pirithoüs had sped
490 So well with her, that they shall wed:
He was the happiest of men.
His wedding-day drew near; and then,
To please his love, and gladden her,
He bade – by note or messenger –

* This story is from Ovid's *Metamorphoses*, Book Twelve. I have,
for my own convenience, adopted the alternative form 'Hippo-
damë' instead of the more usual 'Hippodamia'.

His friends to banquet with them. And
With all the pomp at his command,
The two young people were espoused.
When all the guests were safely housed,
And were at table feasting, there
Was wine in plenty, and to spare,   500
Of every kind a man could ask:
But it was Bacchus broached the cask;
All in the party, more or less,
Were overcome by drunkenness,
And left their wits within the cup.
And Venus too had taken up
The cause which Bacchus had begun:
She poured a draught for everyone,
Of that strong vintage which excites
The lust wherein mankind delights.   510
So, all of them in two ways drunk,
That little spark of tinder-spunk
Named lust made all of them half-mad;
They lost such reason as they had,
And had no eyes for anything
But her – the maid whose marrying
They all had witnessed earlier:
That fresh and frolic bride, on her
It was, they turned their every thought.
Then, satisfaction must be sought   520
For all this lust; half-man, half-beast,
Centaurs had mingled in the feast:
With one assent, with one accord,
They stole the lady from her lord,
And bore her off with them, in rage
Of lust which nothing could assuage.
Drunkenness was the cause of this –
And has led many a man amiss
In love, as well as t'other way;
Whereof I shall have more to say: 530
It is the nature of this sin,

By custom, use, and origin,
That it is deadly to Man's grace.
There is a tale, which, in its place
And time, had truth, and thou shalt hear,
Of fools who made such drunken cheer.

[*This is the story of Galba and Vitellius. They jointly ruled
Spain, and were both great drunkards. They ravished both
wives and maidens, but were at last brought to justice and con-
demned to death. Accordingly, they filled a huge bowl full of
wine, and drank until they were senseless; then, already half-
dead, they were slain. So to the second kind of Gluttony, which
is called Delicacy, or Daintiness. This also is a servant of
Venus, and will often, furthermore, destroy a man's health.*]

CONFESSOR:

He who in Love is delicate
May also find his health abate:
Though he may have beneath his hand
The finest wife in all the land,
Or the most lovely love of all,
670   Yet soon his appetite will fall
On others more delicious to
His fancy than the lady who
Is in his house; and many are thus:
Let them be warnings unto us.
Now look at it another way:
Full often I have heard men say
That he whose lust has been denied
Is angry and dissatisfied,
Although his lady be as kind
680   As, with a clear and quiet mind,
Will save her honour and good name.
He wants the whole hog, all the same;
Careless of causing her distress,
His love turns all to daintiness;
Her kindness gives him no delight;

He must fulfil his appetite.
My son, if thou hast acted so,
Tell me.

GOWER:

My holy father, no.
I never yet was delicate
In such a manner as you state,   690
As touching love, in all my life.
For if I had the sort of wife
That you describe, what more were there
To ask for? I should never care,
By her alone my heart being fed,
To lust for a new maidenhead;
And if I did, it were a waste.
As yet, though, I might never taste
Such joys as you describe above,
In wife nor any other love.   700
Never a crumb is given me:
On Lenten diet, as you see,
I am in every season fed;
My heart goes supperless to bed.
If I might have no more than you
Describe, and that my Lady threw
Me crusts of kindness once or twice,
Even that little would suffice,
For some while, as my aliment;
I would not be so ill-content.   710
But by my soul, good father, she
Does no such thing; it seems to me
That even were I sure to die,
She would not turn aside her eye
To feed with one small kindly look
My starving heart: with such a cook
A man might fast for ever more.
But if she has some pain in store,
With which to make a man's heart fat,

720 At every meal she serves me *that*,
Long after I have cried 'Enough' –
And yet such victuals are so tough
They bring my stomach to distress.
Well, such is the Love-Daintiness
(No more) with which my heart must feed;
Thus do I lack what most I need.

Nevertheless, I cannot say
That I am guiltless, every way,
Of Delicacy: were I so,
730 My forces would indeed be low;
A moment's pleasure, now and then,
Does ease and comfort me again;
I find a little love-food there.
For though I may not fully share
Love's banquet, yet I can and may
Find lesser pleasures that allay
My hunger; so I hunt for these,
And for a while they give me ease.
Do you know, father, what I mean?

CONFESSOR:

740 Good son, make thy confession clean,
And say what cates thou hast pursued,
Whereof thine heart obtains its food.

GOWER:

Good father, you must bear in mind
That each is of a different kind;
And, of these dainties, there are three.
The first derives from what I see;
The second comes from what I hear;
The third, as shortly shall appear,
Springs wholly from my inner thought:
750 Without them I would come to naught;
For, when the heart's provider fails,

Death enters after, and prevails.

First of these dainties, then, is sight,
From which mine eye, in all delight,
Receives the kind of food which is
Sufficient and by nature his.
When I am walking to that place
Where I shall see my lady's face,
These eyes of mine – so loth to fast –
Begin to hunger; one hour passed   760
Without her, seem to them like three,
Till – there I am, and there is she:
And then they have such appetite
To feast upon her, such delight,
No other dainty do they need.
Many the sights on which they feed:
They see her countenance, in hue
Fresher than ever flower blew;
They see her forehead – oh how broad
And smooth it is, and how unflawed!   770
They see her nose, how straight it lies,
And the wide heaven of her eyes;
Her cheeks, the colour of the rose,
And her sweet lips more red than those.
All that they see is full of grace:
Her chin, that so adorns her face;
Her neck, so slender, pure, and round –
No sign of bone or wrinkle found;
Her hands, so delicate and white.
I may observe, and guiltless quite,   780
Such naked loveliness at least;
And it is not a meagre feast:
Delicacy it is indeed,
On which these eyes of mine may feed,
When they may see her body, all
So rounded, and her waist so small,
Her aspect and her fair array

More pleasant than the month of May
Full-clad among its melting showers
790   And rainbow gaiety of flowers.

[*If all my other senses agreed with my sight, Gower says, I
would stand before my lady for ever. But they must be satisfied
too.*]

GOWER:

Sight failing, then my ear will serve –
And, from my heart, great thanks deserve
For feeding him from day to day
With every dainty that he may.
Because it seems that everywhere
I wander, all the people there
Will laud my lady to the skies:
Thus, one man says that she is wise;
Another says that she is good;
840   Yet others praise the noble blood
From which she springs, or will declare
Her beauty is beyond compare;
Others commend her graciousness:
No words I hear, but they express
Some commendation of my dear.
This is a banquet to my ear.
It feasts on other dainties too;
For if, as now and then I do,
I hear what she herself has spoken,
850   At once I count my long fast broken:
Her every word is utterly
Instinct with faith and honesty –
And of such comfortable cheer,
It is most soothing to my ear;
No Lombard* ever baked a dish
More dainty to my dearest wish,
For all his condiments and meats;
Nor can he nourish, with those sweets

* Lombard cooks were almost as famous as Lombard bankers.

Of his, so long and heartily
As – by my life and liberty –   860
Do the least phrases from her mouth.
For, as the breezes of the South
Are gentler than all winds that waft,
So, when her speech is kind and soft,
Such virtue lies in speech so calm,
It heals my heartache like a balm.
And should she chance, among the throng,
To carol out some little song,
I listen to it hungrily,
Led into such an ecstasy,   870
I think myself in Paradise;
For truly, when the tones arise
Of that sweet voice, the blissful sound
Seems to build heaven all around.

[*His ear has other consolations too, such as listening to the
stories of old-time lovers. These make him think that sorrow
does not endure for ever; and, for a while, he feels hope –*
    Though hope itself will stay with me
    *No longer than a Cherry Fair.**
*To sight and hearing, a third pleasure joins its forces; and
Gower now describes it.*]

GOWER:

And when I lie alone at night,
Starved of the pleasures of the sight,
When all is silent as the tomb,
Then he stands ready in my room   910
To bring my reresouper† to me,
And feed my heart, if that may be.
This lusty cook is Thought by name:
Boiling for ever on the flame,
Love's cauldron is kept hot as fire

* A proverbial expression for transient glories or joys.
† A late-night meal, an 'after-supper', taken by revellers.

By him. With fancy and desire
Full oft, ere now, this cook has fed
My heart, when I have been abed;
He sets before me a ragoût
920 Of every sound, and image too,
That gave me joy throughout the day.
Yet this is but a mock array,
My only foods are ifs and wishes:
Though I may gaze upon his dishes,
For all I taste or all I feel
I never yet have had a meal.

[Thus, Gower says, he can hardly be called 'delicate' or gluttonous:

I lick my honey off the thorn;
I work my jaws upon my bridle ...
And live, as plovers do, on air.

Genius exonerates him from any grave sin, but tells him the story of Dives and Lazarus.]

CONFESSOR:

A mighty lord of great estate
There was, who was so delicate
In clothing, that he made him gay
990 In lawn and purple every day;
And he would eat and drink his fill
After the pleasures of his will –
Like one who, wrapped in luxury,
Gives not a fig for gluttony.
It happened that a leper stood,
One day, before his gate; and food
Was all the unhappy wretch's prayer.
He did not get a morsel there,
To keep his dreadful hunger still;
1000 That other, who had gorged his fill
On all the pleasures of the board,
Deigned not to answer, nor afford

224

Even a single crumb whereby
The wretched leper might not die
But live upon his charity.
The beggar lay in misery,
Frozen and starved, at Dives' door –
For he could rise and walk no more,
He was in such a sorry state.
Then, as the Holy Books relate,   1010
The hounds came pacing from the hall
To where his plague had made him fall;
And, pitying him, to give him ease,
They licked the wounds of his disease,
There on Death's threshold as he lay.
But nothing could keep death away,
He was so leprous and unfed.
The soul from out the body fled;
It was ordained upon that hour
By Him, almighty in His power,   1020
Our peerless Lord, that he should rise
To the sweet courts of Paradise,
In Abraham's bosom there to lie
And taste the joys of the Most High,
And have whatever he desired.

It happened now, as God required,
That the rich man, within a breath,
Was overthrown by sudden death;
Nor found he any twist or turn:
To hell he must, and there must burn.   1030
The Devil dragged him in; and there
Was pain in plenty, and to spare,
Among those flames that never cease.
Rolling his eyes to seek release,
He cast his glance up to the sky;
And there above him could descry,
Just on the farthest edge of sight,
Lazarus all enthroned and bright,

Beside the Patriarch. So, straightway,
1040 To Abraham he began to pray:
'Make Lazarus leave his seat, descend,
And merely wet his finger-end
And let me suck the water-drop
Upon my tongue, that I may stop
This dreadful heat in which I burn.'
Then Abraham answered, in his turn,
And gave him words to this effect:
'My son, it fits thee to reflect,
And to remember evermore,
1050 The penance Lazarus did was sore
While soul and body were still wed –
While thou towards fleshly pleasure sped,
And lived in luxury and mirth.
And therefore, all thou didst on Earth
Shall be requited thee again:
Thy wages are the deadly pain
Of Hell, for all eternity.
This Lazarus has finally
Outsoared the Earth's dominion
1060 Of pain; his life has now begun
In heaven's joy that has no end.
As to thy prayer, that I should send
Down Lazarus, with his finger-tip
Made moist, that he might let thee sip,
And cool thy burning tongue: learn well
That no such mercies reach to hell;
For unto that foul pit of sin
Thou hast eternal dwelling in,
We may no more descend than thou
1070 Canst clamber into Heaven now;
There is a gulf between us two.'

Then Dives cried to him anew:
'O Abraham! if thus it be,
That Lazarus may not bring to me,

What I have prayed for in this place,
Then I will ask a different grace.
Besides my father, I have five
Brothers, and all are still alive,
And in one mansion dwell they all:
I pray thee, let thy mercy fall   1080
On them at least, and Lazarus now
Visit the six to warn them how
This afterlife is using me –
That they in their turn may not be
Subjected to such pain as I.
Ah, this I pray and thus I cry,
Now I myself may not repent.'

And to this prayer the Patriarch sent
Straightway an answer; he said 'Nay':
Was it not true that every day   1090
On Earth his brethren might have read,
Or heard men preach, what Moses said –
And many other prophets too –
Of what was best for men to do?
True, Dives answered; but if thus,
Back from the dead, came Lazarus
With such an awful truth to tell,
Then merely from their fear of hell,
If nothing else, they would pay heed.
But Abraham answered, 'No, indeed;   1100
For if they still do not obey
All those who lead them in the Way
And evermore proclaim and tell
The truths of Heaven and of Hell,
Still they would pay no heed at all
Though it should verily befall
That a dead man should thus return;
No readier would they be, to learn,
Than of a person yet alive.'

BOOK SIX: GLUTTONY

[*The Confessor now leads into the moral of this tale.*]

CONFESSOR:

Thus a rich man, if he be wise,
1130 Within his heart will never prize
The goods of this world: he may use
All wealth, but rule it; may refuse
No good, but govern everything.
Bangle and brooch and regal ring,
And cloth of gold, and jewellery
He takes – but not in delicacy –
And freely will he wear all this.
The most luxurious food there is,
He swallows, and the richest wine;
1140 But though his meat and drink be fine,
We may not call him gluttonous;
The road he runs is virtuous:
He feeds and clothes his body, true,
But caters for the spirit too.

[*We now hear the story of Nero's 'delicacy'. All his desires –
for food, drink, and women – were unnatural or inordinate. On
one occasion, wishing to know how his stomach worked, he
summoned three men to a banquet. When they had eaten and
drunk their fill, he made one of them ride vigorously, one walk
gently, one sleep. He then cut them open to see which of them
had digested best: it was the man who had gently walked about.**
The Confessor turns now to the use of sorcery and witchcraft.*]

CONFESSOR:

Who dares attempt what Love dares not?
For laws, he never cares a jot,
Except his own; and yet his wish
Is law to bird and beast and fish –
And man himself. All creatures bow

---

* The story of Nero's experiment is told also of Frederick II
Hohenstaufen.

To Love, whom none may daunt or cow.
Enthroned within the hearts of men,
He never takes into his ken
Either their welfare or their ill;
Little he recks of warm or chill,   1270
Little he recks of wet or dry,
Nor who may live, nor who may die;
Neither before nor yet behind
He looks; but, like the inly blind,
Eyeless of spirit, in this fashion
He works the wonders of his passion.
If there is aught that he would draw
Towards him, farewell God and Law;
He cannot recognize their force;
But like Bayard, the blinded horse,   1280
He answers no man's hand at all
Till plump into the ditch they fall;
Is so rebellious to rule,
No skill can make him go to school.
To say what is no more than true,
Full many a marvel will he do
That might be better left undone:
The witch's evil craft is one,
By certain men called Sorcery;
To gain the ends of gallantry,   1290
There have been lovers who would use
All means that godly hearts refuse.

[*We are now given a dissertation upon the Magic Arts –
obviously derived from the writings of Albertus Magnus. It was
Saturn who first, by making marks in sand, invented Geomancy.
With water, Hydromancy is practised; with fire, Pyromancy;
and with air, Aeromancy. These are not necessarily evil in
themselves, unlike Necromancy. There follows a list of eminent
magicians, and a description of 'natural' magic which depends
upon the stars and the elements.*

Gower denies having practised magic in pursuit of his love,

*but confesses that he might well have been tempted. He is
warned that misfortune always follows the practice of the Black
Arts; and the Confessor cites two stories as proof. The first
of these is that of Ulysses.*]

CONFESSOR:

Now, he was a great rhetorician,
And also a profound magician;
For he had made himself the master
Of Cicero and Zoroaster,
Of Ptolemy's astronomy
And Plato's deep philosophy;
Like Daniel, read sleepy dreams;
And knew all Neptune's water-streams;
Knew Macer's Herbal, and had gone
For proverbs to King Solomon,
For medicine to Hippocrates;
Pythagorean subtleties
Of surgery, full well he knew.
And now I shall recount a few
Of his adventures – which, my son,
Will show what Sorcery has done.

This King whom I have mentioned, then,*
Was sailing home from Troy again,
Through many a high and stormy sea;
Gales and head-winds encountered he,
But, in his wisdom, could contrive
To pass all perils, and survive.
Nevertheless, it should be known,
In spite of needle and of stone,
The tempest hurled him suddenly
Upon the strand of Sicily;

1400

1410

1420

---

* This version of the story is in part from the *Roman de Troie*, in
part from *Metamorphoses*, Book Fourteen. In the classical version,
Circe and Calypso did not, of course, both occupy Sicily, but the
islands of Aeaea and Ogygia, respectively.

And there he must remain awhile.
There were two queens that ruled the isle,
Called Circe and Calypso: they
Heard how the King was castaway,
With all his men, upon their shore;
At once they sent for him, therefore;   1430
With a few soldiers, picked by name,
Into their court Ulysses came.

The queens were demi-goddesses,
And skilled in evil sorceries;
Whatever stranger touched their isle,
That lord they would so misbeguile
Into wild lust, and fool him so,
That he would never look to go
Till they had all that he possessed.
All this the wise Ulysses guessed: 1440
If they knew much, he knew much more.
They used against him all their lore,
And worked with many a subtle wile;
But him they never could beguile.
The greater part, though, of his crew,
They mastered – and transformed them to
Creatures obsequious to their word:
Some into swine, a filthy herd;
Some into other beasts or fowls,
As bears or tigers, apes or owls,   1450
And sundry creatures which must do
All that the queens adjured them to
By more-than-mortal sorcery.
Yet they could find no subtlety
By which Ulysses could be caught;
He turned their magic arts to naught;
And he himself wove such a spell
That deep in love with *him* they fell.
Strong in the science of his art,
So well Ulysses played his part   1460

(Sober himself, they driven wild),
That Circe found herself with child.
Thus did Ulysses tame them both;
And, whether they were lief or loth,
Stole all their wealth and their devotion,
And made off safely to the ocean:
Circe may hug her swollen sides,
Ulysses waits upon the tides,
And, straight across the salt-sea foam,
Steers for Penelope and home.

[*All is not well, however. Ulysses is warned in a dream that his
son will kill him. Sure enough, Telegonus – the offspring of
that sorcerous union – at last compasses his death. Such are the
punishments of witchcraft and adultery. A similar story is told
of the magician-king of Egypt, Nectanabis.* Beset by his
enemies, he fled to Macedonia. There he used his magic arts
upon Queen Olympias, and Philip her husband, to persuade
them that the Egyptian god Amos (?Amon) wished to lie with
her and beget a son. She consented; but her visitor was of course
Nectanabis himself.*]

CONFESSOR:

In fair nativity her child
Was born; and, close upon it, there
2260   Were signs and portents everywhere:
Earthquakes made all the welkin reel;
The Sun took on the hue of steel,
And lost his light; winds, fierce and cold,
Blew down full many a tower and hold;
The sea grew eerie, full of change,
The face of all the world was strange;
Wild fire and threatening thunder-crack
So raged amid the Zodiac
That every creature upon Earth

* Gower bases his tale upon the *Roman de Toute Chevalerie*, by
Eustace of Kent, and upon the *Historia Alexandri de Preliis*.

Counted his life but little worth.

[*The child is called Alexander, and is instructed in astronomy
by Nectanabis himself; in philosophy, by Aristotle. One day,
on a high tower, Nectanabis is instructing Alexander in star-
craft, and prophesies that he himself will be slain by his son.
To disprove this, Alexander pushes him off the tower – which
is in itself the fulfilment of the prophecy: serve him right, for
misusing – or using at all – his magic powers. Zoroaster and
Saul are further examples of men who were punished for
employing sorcery.*

    *Book Six ends with a request from the Lover that Genius
should tell him precisely how Aristotle educated Alexander.
This the Confessor undertakes to do.*]

Book Seven: The Education of a King*

[*Genius introduces his promised account of the education of Alexander by Aristotle. There are, he says, three main branches of Philosophy: Theoric, Rhetoric, and Practic. Theoric is itself divided into three parts, the first of which is Theology. The others are Physics and Mathematics. Theology is concerned with divine and spiritual matters; Physic, with the properties of temporal and corporeal things – such as animals, plants, stones, and Man himself; Mathematics is further divided into Arithmetic, Music, Geometry, and Astronomy. All this, declares Genius, Aristotle taught to Alexander.*

Next, Alexander learnt about the creation of the four Elements from formless universal matter. These are Earth, which is round in shape; Water, which courses through Earth as blood does through our veins; Air, which is divided into three 'peripheries' – that of mist and dew and frost, that of rain, and that of lightning; Fire, which surrounds all the other three.

Similarly, mankind are formed out of four 'complexions': the Melancholic, which corresponds to Earth and is seated in the spleen; the Phlegmatic, which corresponds to Water and is seated in the lungs; the Sanguine, which corresponds to Air and is seated in the liver; the Choleric, which corresponds to Fire, and dwells in the gall. Various admixtures of these determine men's physiques and characters. But the heart rules all of these, and all are inferior to the Soul.

* I have treated much of this book in prose summary, since – though interesting in itself – Gower's Aristotelian lore makes for laborious verse.

The whole of it is, of course, a sidelong glance at Richard II. Gower's masterly handling of the medieval Aristotelian system is partly derived from Brunetto Latini's *Trésor*. The division into Theoric, Rhetoric, and Practic, is equivalent to Aristotle's classification of knowledge into Theoretical, Poetical, and Practical. Gower's subdivisions of the first and third classes also follow Aristotle.

Next we are told of the three continents (Asia, Africa, Europe), and of the seas; and this section is rounded off by the mention of yet a fifth Element – Orbis, or Aether – which is beyond all the rest. So we turn to the first branch of Mathematics; in this case, Astronomy.

All earthly life is governed by the stars and planets; Astronomy is the knowledge of their movement, Astrology of their effects. The fifth element is that in which the heavenly bodies move. There are, first of all, seven Planets. Nearest of these to the Earth is the Moon, which rules the sea and all shellfish. Men born under its influence become great travellers, and it has especial power over Germans and Britons.

Next above the Moon, is Mercury. People born under Mercury are literary, but with a tendency to idleness. It has especial power over France and Burgundy.

After Mercury, comes Venus. This is the lovers' planet; men born under it are joyful, courteous, debonair, persuasive, and very amorous. Lombardy is the land of Venus.]

CONFESSOR:

AFTER this planet ruling love,   801
Stands the bright sun that shines above:
He who is enemy to night,
And fountain of our daily light;
The Eye of all the World is he,
For whom the lusty company
Of morning birds awake and sing,
And the fresh flowers spread and spring,
And the tall trees cast down their shade,
And all men's hearts are joyful made.   810
And scholars labour to express
His riches and his nobleness,
He who is lord of all the sky,
When he is seen enthroned on high.

Of glittering gold on spoke and rim,
The chariot wheels that carry him

235

In that fair seat where he sits crowned
With gold that shining stones surround;
And, if I am to speak of them,
820   The forepart of his diadem
Is ornamented notably
With jewels three, that nobody
Has ever seen on Earth. And this
Is the first stone's name: Licuchis;*
The rest I find recorded thus,
Astrices and Ceramius.
Behind his diadem, I read
In ancient books, there are indeed
Another very lovely three,
830   Each set according to degree:
A Crystal is the first of them
That stand behind his diadem;
A Diamond beyond compare;
And, thirdly – noblest and most fair –
A gemstone called Hydriades.
But other jewels border these;
For, as our learned clerk sets down,
About the side-parts of the crown
There are five more – thus, gem by gem:
840   The Emerald is one of them,
The Jasper and the Dendides,
Jacinth and Heliotrope. All these,
Shining aloft where they are set,
Adorn the Sun's bright coronet –
In such a manner that they spread
His glorious light around his head
Within his kingly chariot.

There draw him, swift as arrow-shot,
Within that regal-glittering dray,
850   According to the laws of Day,

* I have been quite unable to identify the following five – no
doubt imaginary – jewels: Lichuchis, Astrices, Ceramius, Hydriades,
Dendides.

236

Four mighty horses, of which I
Shall give the titles by-and-by:
First, Erythreus,* who is bright
And burning, with a ruddy light;
The second, Aethon, as I read;
And Lampos, the third fiery steed;
The last is Philogea; and
These four bring light upon the land.
So high and swiftly do they run,
But four-and-twenty hours are done   860
While Sun and chariot speed and burn
About the heavens, and return,
Through the tall circles that embrace
All Middle Earth: such is their pace.
And thus the Sun is, once for all,
A planet most imperial:
Above him, and beneath him, three;
And, all among them, King is he:
He lords it in the middle place
Among the Seven; and his face   870
Gladdens all creatures, and gives ease
Or pastime to their companies.

[*Born beneath his influence, men are liberal and good hearted,
subtle, good goldsmiths, and wise. The country of the Sun is
Greece.*

*Above the Sun, stands the warlike planet Mars. He rules
all soldiers, and all fierce and impetuous men. Palestine is the
land most under his influence.*

*Next is Jupiter, who makes men docile and patient, and good
merchants; he brings peace and pleasure, and his land is
Egypt.*

* I have corrected, to their classical forms, the names of these
four horses as given by Gower. As Macaulay notes, they are said
to represent the four divisions of the day, from early morning to
the sun's apparent approach to Earth at evening (Philogea =
Earth-lover).

Last of all comes Saturn – a cold, cruel, malignant planet, which governs the Orient.

All this, Alexander learnt. And after this, he was taught his calendar and the Signs of the Zodiac. There are twelve of these; and their characters are as follows:

Aries, the Ram.* This contains twelve stars. It is hot and dry, and is one of the 'houses' of Mars. The world was created in Aries, whose month is March, and who rules all reptiles.

Taurus, the Bull. He is dry and cold, and is one of the 'houses' of Venus. His month is April, and he contains twenty stars.

Gemini, the Twins. One of the houses of Mercury, rich in stars. May is the month of Gemini.

Cancer, the Crab. He possesses sixteen stars, and is the house of the Moon. He is moist and cold, and his month is June.

Leo, the Lion. He is hot and dry, and his month is July.

Virgo, the Virgin. She is dry and cold, and is the second house of Mercury. Her month is August.

Libra, the Balance, rules September. It is hot and moist, and the second house of Venus.

Scorpio, the Scorpion, is the second house of Mars. His month is October, and he is a great enemy to Venus.

Sagittarius, the Archer, is a Centaur. He is hot and dry, and is Jupiter's first house. November is his month, and he is foe to Mercury.

Capricornus, the Goat, belongs to Saturn, and hates the Moon. December is his own dark month.

Aquarius, the Water-Carrier, is also Saturn's house. Cold, frosty January is his month:

> *When Janus, with his double face,*
> *Sits in the chair that is his place,*
> *And gazes upon either side –*

---

* Aries, Leo, and Sagittarius are fiery by nature (cf. Gower's treatment of the Elements); Taurus, Virgo, Capricornus, being Earthy, are cold and dry; Gemini, Libra, Aquarius, partaking of the Air, are hot and moist; Cancer, Scorpio, Pisces, being Watery, are cold and moist.

Partly upon the wintertide,
And partly to the coming year:
In this month does that sign appear
By nature; and one gift he brings –
The earliest primrose that is Spring's.

Pisces, the Fishes, is the last sign of all. It is cold and moist, the second of Jupiter's houses, and a friend to Venus. Its month is February.

Next, Alexander learned about the fifteen major stars: but here his teacher was Nectanabis (*see Book Six, l. 1789 ff.*). They are as follows:

1. *Aldebaran.* The brightest and biggest of all. In nature it resembles Mars; in 'complexion' (*see above*), Venus. Its stone is the carbuncle, and its plant *anabulla* (which I cannot identify).

2. *Clota,** or the Pleiades. This is cognate with the Moon and Mars. Its stone is crystal; its herb, fennel.

3. *The third is Algol, bright and red;*
   Saturnian, I have heard said,
   His nature is; yet it behoves
   Him take his character from Jove's.
   His stone is Diamond; and for
   His proper herb, the Hellebore
   He takes, a dark and evil plant:
   Thus herb and stone are consonant.

4. *Capella.* This partakes of Saturn and of Jupiter. Stone, sapphire; herb, *marrubium* (unidentified).

5. *Sirius.* A magic and Venerean star. Stone, beryl; herb, savine.

6. *Procyon.* A star compounded of Mars and Mercury. Stone, agate; plant, primrose.

7. *Regulus.* Stone, *gorgonza* (unidentified); plant, 'celidoine' (unidentified).

8. *Ala Corvi* (Crow's Wing): Martian and Saturnian. Stone, onyx; herb, 'lapacia'.

---

* I cannot trace this name – it is not in fact that of any of the Pleiades.

9. *Spica. Mercurial and Venerean; emerald and sage.*

10. *Arcturus. It partakes of the characters of both Jupiter and Mars. Stone, jasper; herb, plantain.*

11. *Venenas (the second star in the tail of the Great Bear: unidentified by name). Lunar and Venerean. Stone, diamond; herb, chicory.*

12. *Alpheta (= Gemma Coronae Borealis). Governed by Scorpio. Stone, topaz; herb, rosemary.*

13. *Cor Scorpionis. Martian and Jovian. Stone, sard; herb, (?) crocus.*

14. *Botercadent (unidentified). Mercurial and Venerean. Stone, chrysolite; herb, savory.*

15. *Cauda Capricorni (the Tail of the Goat; but called by Gower 'the tail of the Scorpion'). Stone, chalcedony; herb, marjoram.*

Now follows a history of Astronomy. So, to the second main branch of Philosophy, Rhetoric.

Only Man has the power of speech, among terrestrial creatures. And the spoken word is so powerful we must beware of misusing it. Next comes Practic.

Practic has three branches, Ethics, Economics, and Policy. All three are necessary to a King: they teach him to control his own morals; to rule his own household; how to order his Kingdom. The first aspect of Policy is Truth.

Truth and Steadfastness are the chief jewels in the crown of a King, and the gold betokens excellence. A story illustrating the supremacy of truth, is that of Zorobabel.* King Darius of Persia was a very wise man; one day he called three Sages to him – Arpaghes, Manachez and Zorobabel† – and set them the question, 'Which is the strongest: wine, woman, or a king?' Arpaghes said, a king, who has the power of life and death. Manachez said, wine – because it can rule everyone's wits.

---

* The tale is based upon III Esdras iii–iv. But Gower has made certain additions.

† Arpaghes and Manachez: these names are not in Esdras. Were they perhaps suggested to Gower by 'Harpagus' and 'Mnascires'? But Manachez does also recall 'Manasseh'.

Zorobabel, however, said woman – because all men are born of
women, kings and vintners alike; all bow to the love of women,
and women can make men desire honour. He proves this by
describing how he had seen the tyrant Cyrus tamed by his
concubine, and by telling the familiar story of Alcestis, wife of
Admetus.]

ZOROBABEL:

When the great Duke Admetus lay
Sick in his bed, and day by day
Men looked for him to be no more,
His wife Alcestis went to implore   1920
Minerva (thinking she deserved
Some help, as one who long had served),
With sacrifices and with prayer,
That – since her lord lay dying there –
The Goddess might relieve his pain
And bring him back to health again.
Lo, thus she prayed and thus she cried,
Until at last a voice replied
That if she would agree to take
The sickness on her, for his sake,   1930
And die herself, then he should live.
Great thanks Alcestis had to give
Minerva: thus the husband's life,
By willing bargain of the wife,
Was purchased with her death. And then,
Contented, she went home again.
Into her husband's room she ran,
And tenderly embraced the man
In both her arms and kissed him there,
And spoke as if she had no care.   1940
Thereafter, in an hour or so,
This noble wife was stricken low,
And died; while he was whole and hale.
By reason, then, how can we fail
To see that, next to God above,

A woman's faith, a woman's love,
In which lies all that is of worth,
Are mightiest here in Middle Earth,
And comfort us in many ways?

[*The next point of Policy is Largesse or Liberality. A King,
like a lover, must avoid both parsimony and prodigality: and
he must spend his own wealth, not that of his subjects. He must
suitably reward those who have done him service, as is proved by
the story of the Emperor Julius and the Poor Knight. This
Knight came before Julius with a lawsuit, but could afford no
advocate. He was assigned one, but again complained – 'When
I fought under you in Africa, I employed no deputy; now you
should undertake my case yourself.' And Julius did so.*

*On the other hand, Kings should use discretion when they
give presents or rewards – neither too much nor too little. And
they must be especially careful not to reward mere flattery,
which is always found about their courts. Several stories prove
to us the evils of flattery. There is that of Diogenes and
Aristippus. These two philosophers went from Carthage to
Athens, in order to study, and then returned home. Aristippus
grew rich as a court-flatterer, but Diogenes was content to
remain a poor student, dwelling by the riverside, near a bridge.*]

CONFESSOR:

2275　Diogenes, upon a day
　　　Within the merry month of May
　　　When roots and herbs are wholesome, went
　　　Into his garden with intent
　　　To gather both legume and beet.
2280　Which presently he meant to eat.
　　　When he had gathered what he needed,
　　　He sat him down, and so proceeded
　　　To wash them in the stream that flowed
　　　Beside his garden, near the road
　　　Which led up to the bridge – as I
　　　Described before. Now, by-and-by,
　　　Up Aristippus rode by chance,

All troops and pomp and circumstance;
And, at the bridge, drew in his rein,
Like one intending to remain: 2290
For, when he cast his eye around,
There sat his friend upon the ground,
Washing the vegetables clean.
That other said, 'Well, Diogene,
Good morning to you, and God speed;
You surely would have little need
To sit there turning over roots,
If you could lick your Prince's boots
And grow a favourite, like me.'
Diogenes said, 'As to thee,   2300
If thou couldst imitate my way
Of turning over roots, I say
That thou wouldst have small need, or less,
Of flattering obsequiousness.'

[*The Romans put down flattery in the following way: whenever
an Emperor went in triumphal procession after a victory, with
four white horses to draw him, and great pomp before and
behind him, a jester sat beside him in his chariot, with orders to
whisper, 'All this glory is transient; know thyself, and hold
fast to justice.' Further, at the enthronement of an Emperor,
masons would come to ask him how he wished his tomb to be
made: this was a medicine for flattery. That it worked, is
proved by a good story about Caesar.*]

CONFESSOR:

Caesar upon his royal throne
Was set, in splendour all his own,   2450
And none like him beneath the skies.
A certain man, to make him wise,
Fell down before him on his knees
And made such humble reverences
As might befit a god on high:
The courtiers greatly wondered why

He should thus worship and adore.
This man arose from off the floor,
And straight up to the throne he hied
2460   And sat himself at Caesar's side
As if they had been peer and peer,
And said, 'If thou who sittest here
Art God, and hast supernal might,
Then I have worshipped thee aright,
As one divine; but otherwise,
If thou art not what this implies,
But art of mortal flesh, like me,
I have the right to sit by thee,
For we are both alike in kind.'

2470   But Caesar answered, 'Thou art blind
And foolish, as thyself hast made
Most plain; for if thy heart is swayed
To think me God, thou dost amiss
To sit beside thy God, like this;
But if I be a man, then too
It is a foolish thing to do –
To cast away unworthily
That which thou ow'st thy Deity,
And worship me, a mortal man.'

*[In any case, flatterers care only for their own good; and, if a
King takes heed of them, he will rule amiss. A story from the
Bible will prove this very readily. (This is the story of Ahab
and Micaiah, from I Kings xxii, ill-told by Gower.) So to the
third point of Policy, which is Justice.]*

CONFESSOR:

What is a realm, unpeopled? What
Are people, merely, who have not
The rule and guidance of a King?
What is a monarch's governing,
If he but rule a lawless land?

244

And who shall take the law in hand   2700
If judges are not just and true?
Consider empires old and new:
In all their long experience
There is no lack of evidence
That men must not abandon law. ....

[*All in a commonwealth, from the humblest to the highest, have
their proper duties. It is the King's duty to direct the laws of the
land; for though he is above them, he must not injure them.
First he must justify himself before God; then he must see
justice done to all his peoples. Take heed of the Emperor
Maximinus,* who inquired so diligently into men's characters
before allowing them to take office; take heed also of Gaius
Fabricius† whom, when he was consul, the Samnites tried to
bribe with a vast sum of gold.*]

CONFESSOR:

Thereon he bade all people look;   2791
A little of the gold he took
And carried to his mouth – in haste,
It seemed, to smell it, or to taste;
Then to his eye, and then his ear,
And said, 'I find no comfort here.'
And then he spoke with scorn of it
To all who stood around – to wit:
'Now, what has gold, to make it thrive?
Not one of all my senses five   2800
Finds interest or delight therein.
I think it is a foolish sin,
When gold can make men covetous.
But he is rich and glorious
Who can both order and subject
Such men as labour to collect
Great store of gold; and in this way:

* Tale is in Godfrey of Viterbo.
† From Valerius Maximus.

With freedom to be just, he may,
Whether his judgements please or gall,
2810   Give equal justice to them all.

[The Emperor Conrad II* ruled so that no judge dared take a bribe. The consul Carmidotirus† killed himself when he accidentally broke his own law by coming armed to the Senate. King Cambyses‡ flayed alive a venal judge, and nailed his skin to the Seat which his son and successor must occupy. Lycurgus§ the Athenian made all the citizens vow to maintain, during his absence, the excellent laws which he had established: then he departed, with the secret intention never to return.

There follows a list of early law-givers, and a repetition of the maxim that kings must rule justly. All this, says Genius, Aristotle taught to Alexander. And so we pass to the fourth point of Policy, which is Pity.

It was pity that moved God to send His Son down to Earth: every subject should reverence his king, and every king avoid cruelty to his people. This is well illustrated by the tale of Codrus, King of Athens, which Gower obtained from Valerius Maximus.]

CONFESSOR:

Marching against the Dorians,
He thought he would subject his plans
Of battle, and their probable
Results, to the one oracle –
Apollo – that he trusted. By
3190   That oracle, came this reply:
Between two outcomes, he must choose:
To give his body up, and lose
His own life on the battlefield;

---

* From Godfrey of Viterbo.
† From Valerius Maximus – where, however, the consul's name is given as Charondas.
‡ This tale also is in Valerius Maximus.
§ From the *Gesta Romanorum*.

Or to see Athens fall and yield,
If thus he chose, and be subjected.
Pity, in him, had been perfected,
A faith to follow and to cherish:
Rather than see his people perish,
He would himself be slain, he said.
Where now shall men find such a head   3200
As dies to keep the limbs alive?

[*Pompey,* having defeated the King of Armenia, had pity upon him and restored his crown again.*

The opposite of Pity is tyrannous Cruelty, which a King must eschew. Leontius, for example, cruelly served Justinian II — only, himself, to be thus treated by Tiberius, and Justinian reinstated. King Phalaris† of Sicily caused Perillus to make a brazen bull in which men could be roasted to death — their cries, by devilish art, being transformed into a bull's bellowing. Perillus himself was the first to suffer this death. The tyrant Dionysius‡ fed his horses on the flesh of men, but was slain by Hercules. Lichaon§ used to kill and devour his guests, and was turned into a wolf. Thus, tyranny is despicable — and the cruel man, in his own need, will receive only cruelty, and perish. There is an emblem of this in natural history.]

CONFESSOR:

Among the beasts, as we shall find,
The Lion is a savage kind,
Rampant and raging after prey;
If any man should cross his way,   3390
That man is dead who dares to fight.
But if that man has but the sleight
To drop forthwith upon his face,

* From *Valerius Maximus*.

† The story is probably from Godfrey of Viterbo. Gower, mistaking the meaning of *Phalaris Siculus* (Sicilian Phalaris), gives the King's name as 'Siculus'.

‡ Confused, by Gower, with 'Diomedes'.

§ From *Metamorphoses*, Book One.

247

And sue for mercy and for grace,
By nature then the Lion's fire
Is damped, and he restrains his ire
Like a wild beast that has been tamed:
He turns away, as if ashamed,
And does the man no evil deed.

3400 How, then, shall any Prince succeed
In worldly matters, if he wields
His power of death on one who yields
Himself, entire, to charity?
One point I make especially:
There have been many, and shall be more,
Tyrants whose hearts no pity bore;
No spark of pity could restrain
Their joy in having others slain,
Nor mitigate their tyranny.

3410 And, as the raging of the sea
Is pitiless when storm-winds blow,
Thus pity cannot halt or slow
The cruel outrage that is part
And parcel of the tyrant's heart –
Engendered there. Of which, I find
A tale has come into my mind.

[*This is the story of Spartachus, which Gower perhaps obtained from Orosius. Spartachus was a soldier king of Persia, and very cruel. Having made war on Queen Thamyris of the Massagetes, and captured her son, he slew the young man. The Queen gathered fresh forces, and ambushed Spartachus, utterly destroying his army. She then filled a vat with the blood of those princes that had served under him, and –*]

CONFESSOR:

She had the tyrant cast therein,
3510 And told him, 'Lo, thy chance to win
Repletion of thine appetite
For blood, which once was thy delight:

248

Now mayst thou drink thy fill of it'.

[*Nevertheless, mercy must not pass all reasonable bounds: a
king must be courageous, and slay when righteousness is at
stake. Else he will call to mind the people in a certain
fable. . . .*]

CONFESSOR:

In olden days it came to pass   3553
That once a certain mountain was
Up in the wilds of Arcady.
Strange and enormous sounds made she,
Because by chance it was the day
When she upon her childbed lay.
And when the throes were on her (whom
All feared, therefore) the crack of doom   3560
Seemed less a matter for men's fears
Than this which clamoured in their ears:
They heard the noise for miles about,
And listened full of fear and doubt
That, when the child had left her, they
Would suffer as on Judgement Day.
Ever the closer came her hour;
And all the while, with swelling power,
The more unbiddably she cried.
When folk were scattered far and wide,   3570
In fear, and empty every house,
She was delivered of a mouse.

[*There are many cases, some of them in the Bible, of men who
have known when it was right – and righteous – to make war;
or to be pitiless in other ways. Gideon, Saul, and Solomon,*
are examples of this, or of its contrary. And Solomon did well in
asking the Lord for wisdom above all other things: for only
wisdom can hold the balance between justice and mercy.*]

* See Judges vii, 1 Samuel xv, and 1 Kings iii–xii, respectively.

CONFESSOR:

A certain chronicle reads thus:
A King of Rome, named Lucius,
Was in his chamber, late one night;
The Household Steward (a great knight),
And also his Lord Chamberlain,
3950   Had both been ordered to remain;
And, by the chimney-piece, all three
Stood and discussed State Policy.
As it so happened, the Court Fool
Sat by the fire, upon a stool,
Holding his bauble, as if playing;
And yet he heard all they were saying,
Who took no heed of him at all.
On various subjects, great and small,
The King asked counsel of those two;
3960   And they replied with all they knew.
After their full arbitrament,
He questioned them to this intent –
In sober earnest, not in whim:
What did his subjects think of him?
When common people used his name,
Was it with praises, or with blame?
All that had met their ears or eyes
He bade them tell, without disguise;
But, by their oath of loyalty,
3970   To speak the truth, and totally.

The Steward first, in answering
The question posed him by the King,
Said (for his purpose was to flatter)
That the King's name, in all this matter,
Was held both good and honourable.
Now, this was very palatable,
But it was not unvarnished truth.
And now the King must ask, forsooth,

The Chamberlain's opinion.
This man – a wise and subtle one –   3980
Had some regard for honesty:
And common folk believed, said he,
That if the Royal Council had
Been wise and true (they thought it bad),
The King himself (such was their creed)
Would be a worthy King indeed.
And thus he partly blamed this thing
Upon the Council, not the King.

The Court Fool, who was listening still,
Took all this in; and, by God's will,   3990
Knew it was not enough by half;
He gave them both a scornful laugh,
Exclaiming, without more ado,
'My Lord and Sire, if that were true –
If you yourself, by nature, were
So wise and good in character –
How should your Counsellors be bad?'

[*This so moved the King that he dismissed his bad counsellors,
appointed new ones, and reformed the Kingdom. We hear next
the story of Rehoboam, from 1 Kings xii, and that of Anto-
ninus Pius, from Godfrey of Viterbo. Antoninus was said by
Scipio to have declared that he would rather preserve one of his
own subjects than slay a thousand of his enemies: mercy,
justice, and wise counsellors, are the bulwarks of kingship.*

*The fifth point of Policy is Chastity. Although the male is
made for the female, it is unnatural for him to pursue more than
one: it is like borrowing another man's plough when one's own
is adequate. Fleshly lust should be kept within bounds. And a
man has no right to blame women for his own inchastity.*]

CONFESSOR:

Within himself he blows the fire;   4273
She, unaware of his desire,

251

Is blameless, and quite innocent.
For if a man, with full intent,
Should drown himself, whom none may halt,
How can the water be at fault?
Or gold, because men covet it?
4280 A man will have his loving fit –
Undriven on the woman's part;
And if he *will* torment his heart,
How can she stop such foolishness?
Even if he has some success
With her, through pity or her grace,
Still it was he who first gave chase:
The women flee, the men pursue.
Thus it is plain, in Reason's view,
Men are the causes, once for all,
4290 Of their own plight, should it befall
(As often) that they are undone.
And yet full many a subtle one
Has made himself a fool, ere this;
For that is what men's weakness is,
And always has been: in such cases
The strongest men fall on their faces.
Now, it is natural for men
To love, but most unnatural when
Love makes a man an idiot:
4300 For if December turns out hot,
July a waste of ice and snow,
The year is crazed, as well we know.
To see man's nature self-betrayed
By mincing folly for a maid,
That is as if a man should do
His stocking on above his shoe,
Leaving all sense and manliness.
The world has often, none the less,
Known mighty Princes who thus erred –
4310 Whom love has led to look absurd,
With all their manhood undermined.

[*Examples follow. The first is Sardanapalus, King of Assyria. He grew so effeminate that he spent all his time among women, and in womanish occupations: he lost both his honour and his Kingdom. King David himself was a great lover, but not so as to neglect his martial and knightly duties. Cyrus, King of Persia, was unable to conquer the Lydians. He made an 'everlasting' peace with them, so that they fell into sloth, luxury, and lechery – whereupon he conquered them easily.*

There is another example in the Bible (Numbers xxii-xxv): that of Balaam, who led the Hebrews to ruin through lust. Solomon himself is a further evil example of what may happen to lustful kings (1 Kings xi): he took wives from many nations, was led astray by them into idolatry, and left a divided kingdom.

A non-biblical example is that of M. Aurelius Antoninus (Caracalla), who paid dearly for his lechery. And an excellent tale in further illustration is that of Tarquin and his son Aruns.

The tyrant Tarquin had many sons, but Aruns* was the one who most resembled him in lust and cruelty. It happened that they were at war with the Gabians; and, one day, Aruns visited the enemy and displayed to them some wounds which he claimed had been given him by his father and brothers, but which were in fact self-inflicted. The Gabians thereupon allowed him to join them as their leader, so that eventually – by treachery – he delivered their city to the Romans. At a solemn sacrifice in the Temple of Phoebus, a hideous serpent appeared from under the altar and devoured the offerings. The God proclaimed that this evil omen came from the wickedness of Tarquin and Aruns; and he who first kissed his mother should avenge all that wickedness. A knight called Brutus kissed the ground at his feet, since the Earth is mother of us all.

---

* This version of the Rape of Lucrece bears comparison with Shakespeare's – and with Chaucer's in *The Legend of Good Women*. Its source is Ovid's *Fasti*. It should be noted, however, that Gower substitutes 'Aruns' (not a name, but an Etruscan title) for the historical Sextus Tarquinius.

*Now, a little later, Tarquin and Aruns were besieging the
town of Ardea.*]

CONFESSOR:

4763 And it so happened that one night
   Aruns bethought him to invite
   A number of his cavalry
   To sup with him in company.
   Supper was ready as they were,
   And as they sat at table there,
   Among full many a mirthful word,
4770 From Aruns a great boast was heard –
   That he possessed the finest wife
   In Rome. And so they fell to strife,
   And would not grant that she was best.
   They quarrelled on, and had no rest,
   Until the worthy Collatine
   (A noble knight of Tarquin's line,
   And Aruns' cousin) said his say:
   'Words will prove nothing either way,'
   He cried. 'The proof a husband heeds,
4780 Lies not in boasting but in deeds.
   There is a swift way of deciding –
   Leaping to horse forthwith, and riding
   To where our wives are. Thus we two
   May, unbeknown, learn what they do:
   This were a true arbitrament.'

   Aruns made no sort of dissent;
   Up on their horses' backs they leapt,
   And rode and rode and never slept
   Until, in secret, they had come
4790 Within the city walls of Rome.
   There, at an inn where no one knew them,
   They took a room; and so withdrew them,
   A little while, until disguise
   Had made them safe from all men's eyes.

Then to the Palace they repaired
To see, first, how that lady fared –
The vaunted wife of Aruns. Her
They found a happy reveller,
All merriment and smiling jest;
But never a word, among the rest,   4800
About her husband at the war.

The watchers need learn nothing more
Of *her* activities; and so,
Still unespied, straightway they go
Forth to the Gate of Brass – that same
Which is Collatia* by name –
Where Collatine has his abode.
At home, within, there sat and sewed
Lucrece, his wife, and none beside
But women round her, occupied   4810
On the same task, as busily.
She bade them haste: 'This is,' said she,
'For wearing by my dearest lord –
He who lies now, with spear and sword,
There at the siege, with little ease.
Oh, if it might my husband please,
Would God that now I had him near;
For certainly, until I hear
Good news of him and how he fares,
My heart will not be free from cares.   4820
For all men witness of him thus:
He is so rashly valorous
That his own welfare counts for naught –
And that is my most anxious thought,
For when they shall assault the Wall.
Ah, if my wishes helped at all,

* This is Gower's misreading of Ovid, who has 'the brazen
gate of Collatia' – the town from which L. Tarquinius Collatinus
derived his title.

The Wall should lie as deep as Hell,
The siege be lifted, all be well,
And Collatine come back to me.'
4830 Her tears began to brim, and she
Had not the heart to wipe her eyes:
And, as on leaf and flower lies
The dripping dew, so now upon
Her white face, the salt teardrops shone
In woeful beauty as they fell.

When Collatine had heard her tell
The feelings of her faithful heart,
He could not keep himself apart,
But ran to her with, 'Oh, my dear,
4840 Do you not see me standing here,
That love and lord for whom you plain?'
Her countenance grew glad again:
In slender arms she clasped her lord,
And her pale beauty was restored
To colours of such loveliness
As none could rival, nor express.

[*Now Aruns grows bitterly jealous. When Collatine and he
have ridden back to the siege, he cannot keep Lucrece from his
thoughts, nor sleep for thinking of her:*

 The features of her lovely face,
 Where Nature had bestowed such grace
 And beauty, soft and womanly,
 That none could stand in rivalry;
 Her yellow hair, in comely tress;
 The seemly order of her dress;
 And how she spoke, and how she moved,
 And how she wept . . .

*So he determines by some stratagem to satisfy his lust for her. He
secretly returns to Rome, and is innocently welcomed and feasted
by her, as her husband's friend.*]

CONFESSOR:

As yet, no word of love spoke he;   4941
But ambushed in the subtlety
Of false though friendly speech, he lay
As tigers, waiting for their prey,
Abide their time in secret lair.
Now, therefore, when the boards were bare,
And supper cleared from out the hall,
He told her he was fit to fall
Asleep, and begged her for a bed.
About the business she sped   4950
With such a will, no trouble spared,
That everything was soon prepared.
She brought him to his room; and so,
Taking her leave, made haste to go
To her own chamber, which lay near.
And certainly she had no fear
Of him, her seeming friend – but foe.
Whereby, there came a world of woe.

For all the tyrant's easy bed,
He often rose, walked, turned his head   4960
To listen with an anxious ear,
Till everyone – it would appear –
Was safe in bed, and sleeping fast.
Then round about himself he cast
His riding-cloak, and he was armed
With a bare sword. She, unalarmed,
Slept on; but with what dreams, God knows.
For, silently, her doorlatch rose
And fell again; none other stirred;
With secret foot he stole, unheard,   4970
Up to the bed in which she slept;
And, of a sudden in he crept
Beside her. Not till she was taken
Between his arms, did she awaken.

Fear, born of her soft womanhood,
Then stopped her voice; but if she could
Have cried, she dared not cry aloud:
For Aruns threatened her, and vowed
That if she should resist or cry
4980   At all, he had a sword near by
To slay both her and all her kin.
Such was the fear he put her in,
That like a lamb when the wolf's teeth
Close on it, thus Lucrece beneath
His hands lay trembling and half-dead,
Naked and swooning, in her bed.
And he, impetuous in his lust,
Did what he would, and what she must.

[*The story now continues along familiar lines. Aruns returns
to the siege. In the morning, weeping and dressed in black,
Lucrece tells her father and Collatine – and the knight Brutus
(see above). Then, unable to bear her dishonour, she kills herself.
Brutus exhibits her body to the people, and tells them all. Out-
raged, they banish both Tarquin and Aruns, for their tyranny
and lechery.*

*There follows the tale of Appius and Virginia. Unlike
Chaucer (who uses the story for his* Doctor of Physic's Tale,
and follows the Roman de la Rose), *Gower took his matter
directly from Livy.*

*Appius Claudius was Governor of Rome, and had set his
heart upon a beautiful young maiden (called Virginia). But
she was betrothed to a worthy and noble knight, and would not
yield to Appius. Now, Virginia's father was at the wars;
seizing his opportunity, Appius persuaded his brother Marcus
to claim her, unlawfully, as his slave. Her father, learning of
this, returned and appealed against her seizure – but vainly.
Seeing no other way of saving her from dishonour, he slew his
daughter. The whole affair so incensed the Romans that they
rose against Appius and deposed him.*

Even in marriage, Chastity is a virtue, as we learn from the

258

story of Sara and Tobias.* Seven husbands, intent only upon their lust, had been strangled on their wedding night by the demon Asmodeus. Tobias, however, when he married her, followed the instructions of the Angel Raphael: he kept the true laws of marriage, and yet had all he desired (because, as Gower does not say explicitly, he spent the first night in prayer).

Gower expresses gratitude for all this instruction, and all these tales, which were what Aristotle taught Alexander. But he wishes to continue his confession.]

GOWER:

Father, for all that you have told,
I give you thanks a thousand-fold;
Still your tales ring upon mine ear.
And yet my heart – that is not here.
For all that I can do, the pain
Of love has come on me again:
No teaching I have had as yet
Could ever make me once forget
One jot of love – and I must keep
Love's Book of Hours unless I sleep.
Not otherwise may I withdraw
From thought of love and of his law.   5420
Therefore, good father, leave the rest
And speak of that which filled my breast
When we began: if there is aught
Concerning love that slipped our thought,
And whereof I need shriving, ask;
I will confess, and make my task
Amendment, if I live so long,
For things undone or things done wrong.

[The Confessor promises to explain to Gower the last of the Seven Sins.]

* From the Apocrypha (Book of Tobit vi–viii).

Book Eight: Lechery*

[*God cast out from Heaven the rebellious Lucifer and his angels. To replace these fallen angels, he created Adam and Eve, and bade them increase and multiply. When they were expelled from Paradise they were still virgin, but soon had two sons and two daughters – Cain, Abel, Calmana, Debora.† At that time, the marriage of brothers and sisters was not unlawful – 'necessity knows no law' – nor was it made so, until the time of Abraham. Even then, it was still lawful for cousins to wed: thus, gradually, the 'prohibited degrees' of kinship grew wider.*]

CONFESSOR:

But though the Pope forbids us, in
His Canon Law, to wed our kin
Within the second or the third –
Though it is Holy Church's word
That bounds our unions with degrees –
150 It is not seldom that one sees
The rage of lechery, today,
Take what it will, and where it may.
For love, which is devoid and bare
Of reason, as all men declare,
When heedlessness and folly fire
Its wild voluptuous desire,
Spares not a thought for kin or kind,

* Gower is in difficulties here: he has already dealt with almost every aspect of Lechery – including (in Book Three) the main subject of the present Book, which turns out to be Incest. This is probably the reason for his very lengthy treatment of the story of Apollonius.

† Calmana and Debora: these names are found not in Genesis but in the *Revelations* of Methodius.

260

Nor calls religion* to its mind:
No: like a cock among the hens,
Or like a stallion of the Fens   160
Who ramps about among the mares,
For good or ill he never cares,
But takes whatever comes to hand.
Son, I would have thee understand
That all such joys deserve our blame:
Therefore, if thou hast done the same,
Or loved in any way like this,
Shrive thee at once, and do not miss.

GOWER:

In God's name, father, no forsooth:
My market holds not such a booth;   170
Never am I so wild a man
That nearest kin, and dearest, can
Inspire that sort of love in me.
Nor any power that I can see
Could make me dote upon a nun:†
For though her love were to be won,
It were but a delusive prize,
And has no value in my eyes.
Yea, question me of this or that,
The truth of my reply is flat: 180
In all this world there is but one
That holds my heart's dominion;
As to all others, I am free.

CONFESSOR:

Now, good my son, full well I see
Thy word stands steady in one place.
Yet count it unto thee as grace,
That thou so cleanly art acquitted

* This is not an exact translation. Gower is referring to the fact that intercourse with a member of an established religious order was treated as incest.
† See preceding note

Of what *some* lovers have committed,
As thou hast often heard me say:
190 Such times of love are thrown away,
And can be only bitter-sweet;
They seem at first a sugared meat,
But in the final, testing, hour,
They are but transient, and sour.

[*Awful examples follow: Caligula deflowered all three of his own sisters, and sent them into exile, for which sin God deprived him of his empire and of his life; Amnon ravished his sister Tamar,* and was slain at Absalom's command; Lot† lay with his daughters, and his descendants came to no good. Therefore, such wickedness must be avoided: and there is another, longer, story to prove it.*

This is the story of Apollonius of Tyre, obtained by Gower partly from the Pantheon *of Godfrey of Viterbo, partly from the* Historia Apollonii Tyrii. *Gower's tale is itself, of course, one source of Shakespeare's* Pericles, Prince of Tyre, *in which Gower appears as Chorus. There are over 1,700 lines of it, mostly undistinguished: a summary, and a few extracts, will suffice.*

King Antiochus was married to a noble Queen; upon her death, his desire alighted upon his daughter, a virgin of peerless beauty. Unable to defend herself, she yielded to his lust; and, though she confided in her nurse, she was forced to repeat the act on many occasions. In order to discourage her many suitors, Antiochus posed a riddle to them: those who failed to answer it would be beheaded. Many died thus. At last Prince Apollonius of Tyre presented himself as a suitor, and the King recited as follows (ll. 405 ff.):

'*I am raised up by felony;
I eat, and eat incessantly,
My mother's flesh; her lord, my sire,
I ever seek with strong desire,
For son he is unto my wife. . . .*'

* From II Samuel xiii.   † From Genesis xix.

Apollonius answered that he plainly saw that the riddle was entirely concerned with Antiochus and his daughter. To avoid being shamed in public, Antiochus put off the young man's fuller answer, saying he would hear it in thirty days. Prince Apollonius feared some treachery; he secretly returned to Tyre, and departed secretly again in a wheat-ship: and desolate indeed were the people of Tyre (ll. 477 ff.):

> Then they did penance, hard and long:
> There was no dancing, and no song,
> But every mirth and melody
> To them was as a malady.
> In all the grief that they must bear,
> Not one of them would cut his hair;
> Dark and funereal was their dress;
> The public stews, the baths no less,
> Were closed and empty all the day;
> None in that city cared to play,
> Nor thought of joy; with one accord
> They all bewailed their absent lord.

In the meantime, Antiochus had sent a man to Tyre with orders to poison Apollonius. Finding him absent, the messenger returned. Apollonius had in fact arrived at Tarsus, and had taken lodgings with a certain Strangulio and his wife Dionysa. Hearing that Antiochus had tried to kill him, he once more fled, but was shipwrecked on the coast of Cyrenaica. Having reached the town of Pentapolis,* he found a great multitude assembled there to watch the Games — the king and queen of the country among them. Apollonius himself took part, and surpassed all others. Eventually the king's daughter fell in love with him, and they were married. Shortly after, news came from Tyre that Antiochus and his daughter were dead: it was safe for Apollonius and his wife to return, though she was now pregnant.]

CONFESSOR:

When they were in mid-ocean, and

* This was in fact an association of *five* towns: Cyren is meant.

No longer within sight of land,
Out of the North appeared a cloud:
1040 The tempest burst on them, and loud
And fearful was the storm-wind's blast.
The welkin was all overcast
With night; the sun was driven under:
And then the hurricane of thunder!
And now both moon and stars enshroud
Themselves in pitchy cloaks of cloud,
And hide the brightness of their eyes.
Now the young princess weeps and cries,
And is not to be comforted,
1050 And travails, and is brought to bed
In the close cabin where she lay.
In bitter grief, and long ere day,
Her husband rose to meet the morrow:
And thus in anguish and in sorrow
She was delivered, all by night,
And lay as dead, in all men's sight.

[*But the child is a girl, and lives. Apollonius grievously laments his wife; but her body must be disposed of. So she is put overboard in a watertight coffin, lined with cloth of gold, and stored with money and jewels so that anyone finding her body may bury it fittingly. In sorrow, Apollonius makes for Tarsus. In fact, the princess is not dead, and is later found and restored to health by a cunning physician. Supposing herself the only survivor of a shipwreck, she becomes a priestess of Diana at Ephesus.*

At Tarsus, Apollonius entrusts his baby daughter – whose name is Thaïsa – to his old hosts Strangulio and Dionysa, and then sails for Tyre. For a while, the couple care for her admirably, and educate her well. But, by the time she is fourteen, she far outshines Dionysa's own daughter – and this makes the mother jealous. She tells her servant to take the girl to the sea shore, and there murder her. Thaïsa's cries, however, arouse a band of pirates, who seize her, carry her to the city of Mitylene,

264

and there sell her to a certain Leonine, a brothel-keeper.]

CONFESSOR:

He had it bruited round about
That any man who would try out
His lust upon her maidenhead,
Should pay cash-down, and soon be sped;　1420
And having thus proclaimed his ware
To all who happened to be there,
Into his brothel she must go:
Small wonder if she wept for woe!
To her, locked in alone, came ten
Or twelve young lustful gentlemen,
One after one; but out they went:
For, by God's grace, the sad lament
She uttered had on them such sway
That neither heart nor power had they　1430
To do her any injury.
Leonine kept his weather-eye
Upon that hoped-for golden fee:
But all in vain; they let her be,
And none thenceforward sought her there.
Of this, her master grew aware
And, knowing her a virgin yet,
Gave orders to his man to get
The business done – to overpower her
And so, against her will, deflower her.　1440
In goes the man; but when he hears
And heeds her woeful plaints and tears,
He fares no better: as things are,
For weeping he is riper far,
Than for the other kind of game.
And thus she saved herself from shame.

[*Eventually she escapes to safety, and continues her education.
Apollonius, meanwhile, believes her dead; but, arriving by
chance in Mitylene, encounters her. All is now joy, and she is*

265

*wedded to the governor of that city. Warned, in a dream, to go
to Ephesus, Apollonius is next re-united with his wife; and all
ends happily:*

> They joy together, and forget
> Old sorrows under pastimes new.
> Grief, with its pale and yellowed hue,
> Becomes a rosy-smiling cheek;
> There is no mirth a man could seek,
> But he may have it if he will.

*So, the Confessor says, righteous love is rewarded, and un-
righteous punished. Gower denies having ever 'lusted like
a beast'; he has never done worse than wish Danger were out
of his lady's way.*

> But all my arts are thrown away;
> Still she rewards me with a 'Nay':
> That syllable can overthrow
> A thousand phrases in a row,
> Chosen as subtly as I can.
> Father, I am a simple man;
> The more I try, the less I get;
> Though I may not forsake them, yet
> To me the ways of Love are dark;
> But you, who are a learned clerk,
> Do understand them, and may teach.
> Therefore, good father, I beseech,
> Say now what path is best for me.

*The Confessor gives little more than counsel of perfection:
follow truth, and labour no more in vain pursuits.*

> Of every joy, the end is pain,
> And every pain is to be fled;
> I see not how it may be said
> That this is anyone's desire.
> The more the log lies in the fire,
> The sooner into ash it tumbles;
> The foot that in the pathway stumbles,
> Full often brings the head as low;
> Love may be blind, and may not know

Where he is going, till he falls:
However, if it so befalls
That he is counselled well, and led,
There is no danger he needs dread.
Counsel is lord of everything
To one who wishes to be King ...
If he but rule his realm amiss
For lack of counsel, is not this
To lose himself? And that is more
Than boatmen losing boat and oar
And all their worldly goods as well ...
Pearls are no more than the pearl shell
To men who cannot say they own
Themselves, and kings are overthrown
For lack of this.
'*Abandon, therefore, the blindness of love, and thou mayst yet*
recover, and live by reason.']

GOWER:

My father, I have heard your tale,
And were to blame if I should fail   2150
To answer you who counsel so;
But you bear nothing of my woe,
To you it is a game: one's heel,
Whatever pain one's heart may feel,
Recks nothing of it. How can I
Hope from love's agony to fly?
You do not feel that amorous pain
Whereof not you, but I, complain.
Oh, it is easy to command:
The roe that freely roams the land   2160
Cares little that the ox at plough
May fret; men often wonder how
Their neighbours can complain so – who,
The roles being changed, would do so too.

[*Accordingly – though expressing his deep gratitude to*
Genius – Gower asks to be allowed to send a formal petition to

Venus. After long debate, Genius promises to act as his courier; and, using tears instead of ink, Gower sits on the grass and writes as follows.]

GOWER:

Against the sickness of love's painful woe
There is no physic strong and sovereign;
My foolish heart it has bewildered so
2220 That wheresoever I wander or remain,
I find it ready to assault again
And ever again my all-defenceless wit:
Thus I seek help, and ask a cure for it.

For if at first to Nature I complain,
Then I shall find all creatures everywhere
Love in their season, and are loved again –
So that although the wren be tiny, there
Is yet a small belovéd in his care.
I have but one desire, that unpossessed:
2230 I am alone, though all things else are blest.

Nature has taught (why, is beyond my wit)
My heart the paths of love; and yet she gives
To me no help or certainty, that it
Shall come safe home: between alternatives
It stands, uncertain if it dies or lives.
For, though my reason struggle with my will,
Yet have I no escape from loving still.

In me the ancient story is repeated –
How Pan, the God of every animal,
2240 Wrestled with love, and by love was defeated:
Forever I wrestle, and ever I lose the fall,
Because my heart has no more strength at all
To stand and bear love's throes: thence be it
    known
How far my reason has been overthrown.*

* 'Throes . . . overthrown.' The pun is almost certainly intended by Gower himself.

He to whom help is needful, let him sue
For help; or else, in helpless need, fare ill:
My wits being searched and cudgelled through
   and through,
And nothing there to help me to my will,
It seems to me I might as well sit still
As ask my lady for relief; and so,   2250
Where I may turn for help, I do not know.

Should I pray Jove himself to make me free
Of that especial barrel of sweet* wine
Which, in his cellar under lock and key
Lies hidden, Fortune fails in her design:
Too sure it is, the bitter draught is mine,
Drained many a time; that which I would,
   I lack;
And, praying, have but the one answer back.

Change, as I see, is ever the world's way –
Loud windy weather turning warm and
   soft,   2260
And even the great moon changing day by
   day,
And humblest things thrown by degrees aloft;
Hideous War, with all his armour doffed,
Grown Peace: unchanging, though, Love's
   cautious pride
And wilful cold.† And so I am denied.

Ovid, that mighty scholar, speaks thereof,
Discussing love in all its circumstance,
And says there is a blindfold God of Love,
Named Cupid: love is in his governance.
His hands may wield full many a fiery lance, 2270
And will to wound, but not to heal, is his:
This, in some part, is what my quarrel is.

* cf. Book Six, l. 330 ff. (in this translation, summarized only, see p. 216).

† 'Cautious pride ... wilful cold.' I have here employed these phrases to translate 'Danger' (See Book One, p. 87, note.)

Ovid says also that, fair Deity,
In Venus' hand lies love's fulfilment; yes,
But not with Saturn in her company.
And under this conjunction,* I would guess,
My love was born – from which my whole
    distress
Shall spring forever, if I fare not well:
Thus, what advice to take, I cannot tell.

2280 Therefore to you, Cupid and Venus both,
With all my heart's obedience, I pray
That if aforetime you were ever wroth
With me, as Love's apprentice, then today
Forgive, and move infortune from my way;
And let my lady nevermore retain
That Danger who is now among her train.

Cupid, thou God and giver of Love's law,
Whose burning arrow set my heart on fire,
Heal me or salve me: either now withdraw
2290 Thy dart, or give the balm that I desire.
To serve thee in thy Court, and have no hire
Though I have ever heeded thy command:
Where, in thy loving Statute, may *that* stand?

Thou, tender Venus, lady of love, and Queen,
I bear no guilt, that thou tormentest me.
Love pines me, and the wound is evergreen,
Yet am I powerless to uproot the tree.
This, then, I beg, as my last word to thee:
Requite the love that I have bought so dear,
2300 Or tell me plainly I must perish here.

[*From this point to the end, Gower himself resumes the main narrative, as at the beginning of Book One.*]

And when, with full deliberation,

* For the meaning of these astrological references, consult Book Seven, pp. 235-7 in this translation.

This my aforesaid supplication
Had been composed, and written too,
As it has been rehearsed to you,
For Venus' and for Cupid's eye:
Genius the Priest then by-and-by
Took charge of it, and forth he went,
My humble message to present
To Venus, and to learn her will.
For my part, I remained there, still,⁣   2310
But only for such little while
As one might use to walk a mile;
Then, all at once, and close at hand,
I saw the Goddess Venus stand.
In duty bound, beneath a tree,
To earth I bent my humble knee,
And prayed that she would give me grace.
She turned her eyes upon my face –
Half, as it seemed to me, in game –
And asked me what might be my name.   2320
'Madame,' I said, 'it is John Gower.'
'Now, John,' she said, 'unto my power
Thou in thy love must make submission;
For I have read through thy petition
In which to Cupid and to me
Thou hast complained in some degree,
And somewhat unto Nature – though
There I am powerless, thou must know;
That quarrel is between you two:
All sublunary creatures do   2330
Her living homage, in their kind,
Unless, maybe, she chance to find
Some holy man who can withdraw
His instincts from beneath her law;
But that is only now and then:
We do not often see such men.
Plenty enough there are, of those
Whose own perverted pleasure goes

Counter to Nature and her Court,
2340 Enjoying sin of every sort –
As she has many a time complained.
In my Court too they are disdained,
And ever shall be: we receive
None with false colours on their sleeve;
For my Court stands by noble love
Alone, and there is none above,
And none are of my retinue
But them whose love is Nature's due:
Her enemies are not admitted.
2350 Of this, be sure, thou art acquitted;
For thou hast been, this many a year,
One fully licensed to appear
Within my Court, and serve me there:
It should be my especial care,
Therefore, to heed thy sore distress,
And remedy that lucklessness
By which thou hast so long been grieved.
Let, then, my judgement be believed:
Thou shalt be cured, before I go,
2360 Of that unhappy pleasing woe
With which thou sayst thy heart is fired.
But as to *all* thou hast required,
In the main body of thy Bill,
Therein submit thee to my will,
And I will give the matter thought.
Enough, then, if thy cure be wrought:
My physic is both free and strong,
For all, like thee, who suffer long –
Not, haply, what thou wouldst desire,
2370 But such as Reason would require,
And natural in true love's sight.
And as for this thy sorry plight,
Thou shalt be properly rewarded
With what my own Court has accorded:
And if thou cravest more from me,

It is inordinate of thee.'

Venus, obedient to no law
But that of hazard – as men draw
From Ragman Rolls* by chance – will lay
Within her balance, there to weigh,   2380
Only such weights as she may choose;
True-hearted men will often lose
That grace which they have begged of her,
And fortune crown the cozener:
She judges all the world, I find,
In love-suits, as if she were blind.
I do not know what others feel;
It seems that I, on Fortune's wheel,
And I alone, must fill the place
Of one deprived of Venus' grace.   2390
I ask no proof of other men:
She who is called The Goddess then
Set out before mine eyes the end –
Whichever way my love should tend –
That I must dwell in evermore.
When she had eyed me well, she wore
A look half-scornful; thus said she:
'That I am Venus, is to thee
Well known, and that my one desire
Is joy – of which, shouldst thou require   2400
My love, I tell thee plainly, Son,
Within thy person I find none.
For joy of love and hoar-frost hair
Sit ill together anywhere;

* As Macaulay indicates in his note upon this phrase, the
reference is not to the Ragman Rolls proper. There was a species
of game based upon unrelated stanzas, previously composed,
which were drawn for, unseen, and read out to the company (the
amusement lying in their complimentary, or uncomplimentary,
relevance to the reader). Such collections were punningly known
as Ragman Rolls – in reference partly to the true Rolls, partly to
their disconnected brevity. They have given us the modern word
'rigmarole'.

And though thou feignest a young heart,
Thy countenance shows what thou art:
That grizzled horse is not a foal.
They were not few, the years that stole
By thee – and like thee, many more –
2410 While youth was painted on thy door
Though all within grew dull and stale.
"A willing heart, and limbs that fail"
Is a poor motto nowadays.
Beware of making new forays
On love, and failing in the feat;
Better an orderly retreat.
For though thou mightest love attain,
Yet it were but an idle pain,
When thy best powers are too scant
2420 To hold him to his covenant.
And so, take home thy heart again,
Lest – if thou labourest on in vain,
Thou disappoint my Court and me.
I grant thee, and full well I see,
Thou art a willing labourer;
But strength to make the ploughshare stir
Is what thou lackest, in my eyes:
So it behoves thee recognize
Thy weakness, rather than begin
2430 A struggle which thou canst not win.
What bargain should a man essay
Who has not wherewithal to pay?
Take heed, my son, for this is what
Concerns thee; and forget it not:
Instead of "is", write now, "has been":
That grass which once was fresh and green
Has long since turned to withered hay.
Thou askest counsel; and I say,
Remember well that thou art old.'

2440 There fell on me a sudden cold,

When Venus had done speaking, and
I had begun to understand;
Beyond all doubt, I knew for sure,
I could not hope for any cure;
And as a man puts out a fire
With water, thus died my desire:
For grief of heart, my senses failed;
As if in death, my visage paled;
Swooning, I fell to earth. Straightway
It seemed, as helpless there I lay   2450
Neither alive nor fully dead,
That I could see, beside my head,
Where Cupid stood, his bow all bent:
And, as it were, a parliament
Expressly summoned for the nonce,
And seeming all the world at once,
Of gentle folk who formerly
Were lovers. Many a company
Came forth with Cupid, on that ground.
And as I cast my glance around   2460
To learn of them who might be who,
There vigorous Youth stood in my view:
Leader and captain, he stood out
Before all others of that rout
Upon the plain in seemly row.
Their locks were sleek, and all aglow
With many-coloured diadems
Of leaves and flowers and of gems,
Or huge and orient pearls – the while,
All in the new Bohemian* style,   2470
With many a skilful ornament
Made gay and curious, they went
Proudly and joyfully along.
Nor did they miss a single song
About the loves of maid and man,

* This refers to Richard II's marriage, in 1382, to Anne of
Bohemia – when such new fashions were introduced at Court.

Or mirth such as was piped by Pan:
So bravely rang that company
With every kind of minstrelsy,
A man might think that all the wide
2480   Heavens harmoniously cried;
And with such concord came they on,
Of cornemuse and clarion,
Bombard and shawm, played loud and clear,
That such a happy noise to hear
Was half enough to make me whole.
As thus I thought within my soul,
I watched them nimbly dance and leap,
The festival of Love to keep
As youth and pleasure both command,
2490   There was delight on every hand:
They never ceased to laugh and play
And thrust old Sorrow from their way –
For *him* they had no room at all.
I noticed further, I recall,
As far as my poor ears could reach,
The chiefest matters of their speech
Were chivalry, and war's alarms,
And what it is to lie in arms
Of love, when all has been achieved. . . .

[*And now Gower looks back over his vast poem, and gathers it together: for in this company of young lovers, were all whose tales he has told – and others too: Tristram and Yseult, Lancelot and Guinevere, Hercules and Iolë, Paris and Helen, Troilus and Cressida, and many more, all rejoicing. Some, however, lamented now and then – such as Narcissus, Pyramus, Dido, Ariadne, Philomela and Procne, Canace, Achilles and Agamemnon. Lastly, there were four women whom everyone commended above all the rest. These were the four paragons among wives: Penelope, Lucrece, Alcestis, and Halcyone.*

    But now another company approached. . . .]

Age crossed the green, with gentle pace,
Towards Venus in her royal place;
He led great companies, in truth,
But fewer than had followed Youth –   2670
And most were very elderly,
As, by their faces, one might see:
And yet they tried, in all men's sight,
To look as youthful as they might.
But still, there were no pipes to hear,
That might enchant the listener's ear:
Only such music as men know
Befits old age, being soft and low –
The sounds of citole, harp, and lute,
Hove-dance and carol:* tones that suit   2680
Such men, by Love's command and pleasure.
And so they trod a gentle measure –
And sometimes, in a sober style,
Upon their ladies they would smile;
But open laughter there was none.
Still it was plain that every one
Found far more mirth was to be had
In quiet love that made them glad.
Among these dancers I could see
King David, beside Bethsabee;†   2690
And Solomon, there is no doubt,
And with him hundreds in one rout
Of wives and concubines as well,
Hebrew, Islamic, infidel,
Each ready at his beck and call.
I know not how he pleased them all;
Nevertheless, for all his wit,
He had been summoned by that writ
To which Love puts his hand and seal,

---

* The hove-dance was a slow and stately court dance; 'carol'
here means a type of round-dance, accompanied by song.
† The Vulgate form of Bath-sheba (II Samuel xi).

2700 From which no human may appeal.
Also, of course (he mantled in
His trophy, that great lion skin)
Delilah and her dupe I knew,
Strong Samson whom Love overthrew.
And Aristotle, whom the Queen
Of Greece once bridled, there was seen:
Then what a syllogism she
Expounded to him! – so that he
Lost all his logic on that day,

2710 Nor could his art or praxis stay
The power of her argument:
Head over heels in love he went,
And paid the homage that was due.
I recognized great Vergil, too,
Still begging for a kindly word
From that same girl who, I have heard,
Was the Princess of Rome.* Then came
Sortes† and Plato, whom that same
Ovid, our poet, I saw meet.

2720 And then I thought how very sweet
Love was, such wise men to have claimed,
And was myself the less ashamed
And, win or lose, I did not care,
In that misfortune I must bear.
So there I lay, and hoped for grace.
When everyone had reached the place
Where I had fallen at her side,
To Venus all the old men cried
For my sake, mercy to implore.

2730 And she, who could not well ignore

* A reference to the story that the Emperor's daughter once
hung Vergil outside her window, in a box.

† Clearly *not* Socrates, whose name – in its correct form –
appears elsewhere in the poem (e.g. Book Three). Perhaps some
personified magician, suggested by a confusion of the poet
Vergil with Virgil the legendary sorcerer – and with the *Sortes
Vergilianae.*

So great a clamour as they made,
Inclined a pitying ear. She prayed,
However, first, that Cupid would
For his part give me what he could
Of grace, and, of his mercy, send
Some comfort whereby to amend
The grievous plight in which I lay.
And others too began to pray
For mercy, who stood round about –
The old ones chiefly; but the rout   2740
Of youth, all noble courtesy,
Were also heard to pity me. . . .

*[Now a debate begins. Some say Gower is to blame – an old
man besotted by love. Others, that he deserves help:*

*Because, they argued, love's wild rage
Is no respecter of man's age;
If there be oil, and fire be near,
The lamp will then burn high and clear,
And is not easily put out.*

*All this while, Cupid and Venus stand over Gower; and at
last a conclusion is reached.]*

Cupid, because he could not see,   2794
Felt for me with his groping hand
Until he found my body; and,
When he had touched me where I lay,
It seemed to me he plucked away
From the recesses of my heart
His fiery early-planted dart.   2800
Then suddenly he vanished, so
That where he went I do not know,
Nor did a single soul remain,
Of those who followed in his train,
Whom, in my vision, I had seen
Revealed to me – as you have been
Told, not so many lines above.

Quite otherwise, the Queen of Love,
And Genius; for at my side
2810 Awhile, I saw them both abide.
Ere I arose from out my trance,
She who has power to advance
Or to restrain love's action, and
Who bore a boxlet in her hand,
Nor wished to see the death of me,
Took from it – colder than a key –
Some unguent to that end appointed.
My wounded heart was then anointed,
My temples, and my loins; and when
2820 All this was done, she brought me then
A wondrous looking-glass to hold,
And bade me gaze on it; and told
Me, 'Take to heart what you espy.'
Therein we looked, my heart and I:
And oh, how pallid and how grim
I seemed! – such mournful eyes, and dim;
The cheeks grown thin, and all my face
Ravaged with years, in sorry case.
All withered, woe-begone, and shrunken;
2830 Nothing that was not slack and sunken.
But when I saw my frosty hair,
And found no greater pleasure there;
I looked away, in agony.
Then I recalled to memory
My olden days, and times long past,
And Reason rescued me at last:
The times of men, I argued, are
Like twelve months on the calendar,
All of them different, which compose
2840 The year that changes as it goes
Through this or that disparate season.
And thus it is, declared my Reason:
It is at March that we begin,
For then the lusty year comes in;

Strong in his youth, he may remember,
Till August pass, and then September,
His early pleasure and his power,
And grass and leaf, and fruit and flower,
And waving corn and winy grape.
But then the seasons change their shape   2850
To frost and snow, and wind and rain,
Till March once more be come again.
What Summer does the Winter know?
For the green leaves were long ago;
The gay-clad Earth is stripped and bare,
And frozen all her summer-fare;*
All that was warm, has now grown chill.

So thus I thought, and thought my fill;
Till, from the swoon in which I lay,
I roused myself; my wits, astray,   2860
Now I could summon home again.
When, to my Reason, it grew plain
That all my amorous rage had passed,
By the right road he came at last,
And cleansed me of the lunacy
Of that unguided fantasy
Whereof I used so to complain:
Healed of that former fiery pain,
I was as normal as could be.
Then, laughing, Venus looked at me   2870
And asked, as if it were a game,
'What of love now?' And I, for shame,
Could not think how I should reply.
I swore, however, by-and-by,
'I know him not, in God's name; nor
Do my thoughts now approach him, more
Than if my love had never been.'
'John, my good son,' replied Love's Queen,
'Now is the time for thee to know,

* Condition or behaviour appropriate to summer.

2880 Love's Wheel of Luck ran ever so:
I counsel thee, have done with it.'
'Madame,' I said, 'I am not fit –
As, by your leave, is known to you
As surely as I know it too –
From this day forth, to serve within
Your Court. And since I may not win
Your thanks, and now am cast away,
Give me my liberty, I pray.
Nevertheless, and finally,
2890 While I have still my wits with me,
And I have ended all my shrift,
My absolution is the gift
I ask of Genius, ere I go.'
Nor then was my Confessor slow.
He said, 'John Gower, thou art shriven,
And fully pardoned and forgiven.
Forget thy sins, and so will I.'
'My holy father, till I die
I thank you.' Then upon the green
2900 I humbly knelt before the Queen
And begged for leave to go. But she,
To round off all, presented me
With that which I was glad to get:
A rosary as black as jet,
She hung about my neck; all round,
Upon the gauds, these words were found
Spelt out in gold: *Por reposer.**
'John Gower,' she said, 'this shalt thou wear;
Since now thy time is running out,
2910 This comfort I have brought about

* 'Gauds . . . *por reposer*.' The 'gauds' of a rosary were the large
beads (for the Paternosters) at the end of each 'decade'. Since
normally there are either five or ten, the inscription *por reposer*
('to give thee rest') may have circled the rosary twice. Inciden-
tally, I have retained what was clearly Gower's pronunciation of
the phrase: he makes it rhyme with his own name – here, as always
by him, accented on the second syllable.

282

For thee, a lover nevermore.
But I command thee to implore
Continually, now, for peace;
And that thou seek thine own release
From Love, who takes but little heed
Of agéd lovers in their need,
When their delight has had its day.
This, therefore, is the only way:
Take Reason as thy guide – for he
May sadly, soon, misguided be,   2920
Who blindly walks towards dangers. Thou
Must therefore watch thy footsteps now,
And live according to my lore.
Tarry within my Court no more,
But go where moral virtues dwell:
There are those books, I have heard tell,
Whence, all these years, thou drewst thine own.
Take heed, my son, be this well known:
Wouldst thou recover through and through,
Then sue no more, no more pursue,   2930
A quarry thou canst not attain;
It is a senseless thing, and vain,
When such ambitions have their way.
Therefore give ear to what I say;
For, by the laws that guide my reign,
We two must never meet again
From this day forth, thyself and I.
There is no more to say of thy
Dead love, and of thy coming end.
Adieu, for I must now ascend.'   2940
['My poet and disciple greet,   [2940A*]
  Chaucer I mean, when ye shall meet;
  For in his youthful flowery days –

* The sixteen lines that follow are contained in first-recension copies only – e.g. MS. Harleian: 3490. They are inserted here, with 'A' numbering and in square brackets, for the sake of their reference to Chaucer.

As well he could, in many ways –
Where'er I go, I find the land
All filled with joyful ditties and
With songs that he composed for me.
And, therefore, him especially
Do I with gratitude behold.

[2950A] But now that he is growing old,
This be the message thou convey:
That he, in this his latter day,
Being my own most faithful clerk,
On his last work shall now embark,
And write his *Testament of Love**
As thou hast done thy *Shrift*, above.']

2941   And at these words, the starry sky
Enfolded her; she rose on high;
And Venus, who is Queen of Love,
Suddenly sought her Courts above.
There is no more that I can tell
Of her: I bade her then farewell.
And on the instant, Genius
Her Priest, took *his* departure thus:
So – were I lief or were I loth –
2950   Out of my sight they vanished, both.
Then I, left helpless and alone,
Of pride or comfort could find none,
But memories of wasted years,
And sad remorse, and starting tears.
Thus, all my loving gone for naught,
I stood enshrouded in my thought,
And was bewildered for a while.
But then I could not help but smile,
To think of my black rosary
2960   And why it had been given me –
To keep my vigils, and to pray.

* It is pleasant, but not wholly justifiable, to suppose that this may refer to Chaucer's *Legend of Good Women*.

I saw there was no other way:
Now I was utterly rejected,
My way of life must be corrected,
And my old habits used no more.
Full of such thoughts as these, therefore,
Homeward with quiet step I went;
And now henceforth my whole intent,
Since I am shriven, is to give
Myself to prayer while I may live.   2970

[*There follows a review of the condition of England – in tone
and subject, a shorter version of that contained in the Prologue.
It is a prayer for unity, harmony, righteousness, and justice,
within and between all classes of society. Above all, it pleads for
strength and virtue in the King himself:*

    *Whereby, for evermore, his name
    Shall be a blest memorial.*]

And this is my last word of all,
About that work I undertook –
Which was, to write an English book
Half moral and half pleasurable.
I came as near as I was able,   3110
But ask to have its faults excused –
And that it may not be refused
By learned scholars, when they see
Its lack of subtle artistry:
For I have never made pretence
At any skill in eloquence
Or any art to point and pick
My words in forms of rhetoric
Such as we find in Cicero,
But this I say, and this I know,   3120
Although my words be rough and plain,
Yet I have truly taken pain
To keep my promise, and to write
My book. I have done all I might,

As far as sickness would allow.
Also, my days are lengthened now,
And I am weak and impotent:
I know not whither my world went.*
Thus, now being old, my masters all,
3130　I pray, whatever chance befall,
Still in your favour to remain.
For though I lack wherewith to gain
Your worthy thanks by real worth,
Yet my simplicity and dearth
Seek the delight of every lord
Beneath whose governance and ward
I hope in safety to abide.
And now, upon my latter tide,
This book being written, my task done,
3140　My Muse gives her opinion:
She counsels me it shall be best
From this day forth to take my rest,
No more Love's poet. For we know
How many hearts he has brought low,
Or thrown unreasoning and blind.
Among the snares of human-kind.
And there all wisdom goes astray,
And cannot find the proper way
To rule himself in his estate;
3150　But stands forever in debate,
And knows not what he should believe.†

Therefore I take my final leave,
Now at this hour, and evermore –
Of Love and of the deadly sore
He makes, beyond all medicining,
No more to write, no more to sing.
For Love's true nature is perverse,

* Strictly, 'I know not where the world is going'.
† Strictly, 'but, every day, is uncertain within himself, and
cannot mend his ways'.

286

Ever some barrier or some curse
That gives too little or too much:
How may a man delight in such   3160
Pursuits, unless he be no man?
There is another Love, which can
Dwell in his heart unchangingly,
Being sealed in him by Charity.
Such Love is very good to have,
And such Love may the body save,
And such Love may the soul amend:
Such Love may God in Heaven send
Among us, part of all His grace;
So that, above in yonder place,   3170
Where Love abides, and all is rest,
All we may be forever blest.

THE PENGUIN CLASSICS

EDITED BY E. V. RIEU

*

THE MOST RECENT VOLUMES

LACLOS
Les Liaisons Dangereuses · *P. W. K. Stone*

PUSHKIN
The Queen of Spades
and Other Stories · *Rosemary Edmonds*

BHAGAVAD GITA
Juan Mascaró

ZOLA
Thérèse Raquin · *L. W. Tancock*

DANTE
The Divine Comedy – III: Paradise
Dorothy L. Sayers and Barbara Reynolds

ARISTOTLE
Politics · *T. A. Sinclair*

THE LETTERS OF THE YOUNGER PLINY
Betty Radice

JOINVILLE AND VILLEHARDOUIN
Chronicles of the Crusades · *M. R. B. Shaw*

EURIPIDES
Medea and Other Plays · *Philip Vellacott*

BERNAL DÍAZ
The Conquest of New Spain · *J. M. Cohen*

*

A complete list of books is available on application